9-27-65

The Young Disciple

Faustina

Jonah

BOOKS BY PAUL GOODMAN

The Young Disciple, Faustina, Jonah: Three Plays
Making Do
Our Visit to Niagara
The Lordly Hudson and Other Poems
The Empire City
The Break-Up of Our Camp
Parents' Day
Stop-Light and Other Noh Plays
The Facts of Life

*People or Personnel: Decentralizing and the Mixed
    System*
Compulsory Mis-Education
The Society I Live In Is Mine
The Community of Scholars
Utopian Essays and Practical Proposals
Growing Up Absurd
Drawing the Line
Communitas (with Percival Goodman)
Gestalt Therapy (with F. S. Perls and Ralph Hefferline)
Art and Social Nature
Kafka's Prayer
The Structure of Literature

The Young Disciple

Faustina

Jonah

Three Plays

by Paul Goodman

Random House | New York

Jonah originally appeared, in different form, in The Facts of Life, by Paul Goodman, Vanguard Press, Inc.; Faustina was published in the Quarterly Review of Literature.

To L.v.B.
In his 57th year
Deaf no longer

Art of the Theatre

I

It's a play when some do and others watch. What you
needn't watch—for instance, what you can read—is not part
of a play, and too much of it kills a play. But if it needs
more than watching, like answering back or coming to the
rescue, putting it in a play kills *it*.

Artaud, on the contrary, wants the play to come out and
do something *to* the watchers, like a blow or like psychotherapy. But I'd rather have the watchers moved by what
they are doing—watching—I guess I'm not confident enough
in myself to wish to act on other people, no less to do it.
I want accomplices.

Many in the audience are therefore not moved by what
I show, for they *want* to be acted on and manipulated. (I
like it too, within limits.) They don't want to be accomplices, or at least they don't want to be *my* accomplices.

Some playwrights seem to want to persuade the audience
to something, but this is trivial. (Artaud's violence is not
trivial.) What is interesting or true does not persuade, it
moves us from within ourselves like a loved thing, κινεῖ ὡς
ἐρούμενον.

But the common notion is that theatre is illusion, that
what is on the stage is not real and the audience must
believe that it is real. Myself, I never experience this illusion, though I observe that many people do. What is on
the stage is real, it is what is watched. If it tries to deceive,
it is flimsy. Generally speaking, the more illusory it is, the
less interesting to watch.

For instance, I don't like to watch actors, but I am enchanted by watching people act. Actors can't act, only people can act. And when the chips are down and you ask these actors to act out an animal scream, or to let go and tremble, or not to act but just to walk across, they can't imitate anything real or do anything real, for they *are* only actors, theatre-dummies.

It is said that Quintero had to cut the crucial middle scene from *The Balcony* because the actors couldn't stop being "professional."

II

Art moves and teaches—I agree with the neoclassical formula. But art does not move in order to teach, like sugar-coating a pill or seducing. To be moved, watching, *is* to be taught. "Thou art That."

Indeed, with some of us it works the other way: you can move me *if* you teach me. New true sentences open me up to feeling, but feeling never taught me much. (I suppose this is the definition of an intellectual.)

When I make my characters say sentences that I believe to be true, my purpose is not to convince or persuade anybody to anything. It is just that, for me, true sentences have a solid ring, a neat surface, a reliable dynamic, a definite rest. I like their esthetic surface.

I never make a character say something that I know better or could refute, although often I do not *agree* with what he is saying. My characters are at least as shrewd as I am. Otherwise I'd brief them before putting them in the play! But some playwrights run a character through a whole play in order to have him find out what the author knew in the beginning. Why bother?

III

To my taste, the most interesting thing to watch is the everyday, just as it is.

Diaghilev used to say, "Astonish us," but I have no feeling to do this. Anyway, only an impresario would think of it. My experience is that artists find it hard enough just to make sense.

Again, many people like to watch virtuosity, skill beyond adequacy, but I prefer to see amateurs making do, and I am most moved—alas, rarely (I think of Nazimova and Merce Cunningham)—by masterly adequacy. Just as, in love and friendship, I most love the one who *comes across*.

Again, there is something finely theatrical in "camping," exaggerating and decorating something real, as Shakespere usually does and Genet always does; but this too puts me off. I am too puritanical either to like entertainment or to entertain.

When possible, I avoid metaphor, though metaphor may be, as Aristotle says, the essence of poetry. (I don't think it is.) The symbolic I positively detest. Almost always I say it pretty literally as I mean it.

Naturally, it is not always possible to put the real thing on a little stage without artificial helps. But I prefer the audience to *see* the wires by which she is flying. After all, she can't really fly except with wires.

The first plays I ever made were children spinning tops while others play box-ball; a man marking on the wall, inning by inning, the score of a game; a bagpiper, in his outlandish dress, rounding a bend in the park. These pieces were perhaps like what they now call "happenings." But the "happenings" I have seen seem to aim to be eccentric or to shock, whereas I collected ordinary things.

It's not clear to me why I should want to repeat on the stage what the audience can't help but see on the street. Yet why not, if it's pleasant? But I disapprove of retelling remediable evils, which we ought to cope with on the street rather than celebrate on the stage.

IV

Here are examples from the plays in this volume. In *Jonah*, the people sit and have a cup of coffee. (Incidentally they talk and advance the plot, but I don't really care about that.) In *The Young Disciple*, a man is showing a boy how to make a fire with a burning glass, and the tinder ignites with a poof; that's all the scene is supposed to mean. The logic lesson in *Faustina* is similar. Evidently I think that teaching and learning are immensely worth watching, and more important than what is taught or learnt.

The bit of psychotherapy in *Faustina*, when the Emperor plays tiger and the Gladiator realizes that he turns the sword—such a moment is fascinating to me in the clinic or on the stage. And it's good, though pretty unbearable, to watch somebody tremble uncontrolledly, as the young man does in *The Young Disciple*. When he has quieted he can say the poem.

My typical scene of theatre is in the short story "A Ceremonial," where they drop a curtain and disclose a "quiet tree with its heart-shaped leaves and a few cream-colored blossoms in the sunlight."

This tree, at first, excited only wonder, almost disappointment; until it became apparent, just by looking at it, that the utmost tiny leaves and petals were expressive, organs, of the invisible roots. Such as it was, this tree in seclusion had come to its present being, behind a fence. Here it was, this linden tree, when the maroon curtain dropped.

In the story I let this continue for "three or four minutes," which would be vastly too long on the stage.

V

No costumes!—unless it is just the costume, or wearing the costume, that is the deed, the thing to watch. The gorgeous robe of the dancer in the fourth part of a Noh play is itself the *coup de théâtre*; just as in Racine the expected character herself appears and Nero says, *"Dieux!"*

Above all, the stage-set must not sit there, distracting attention to itself for half an hour and an hour. Either let it unobtrusively withdraw or make it function, adjust to the action. Julian Beck of The Living Theater understands this. He learned it, I think, from Cocteau and the Chinese property man; but not from Piscator, whose sets whirl so much that you can't see anything else—they devour you like a German director.

But there is the problem of a curtain, no curtain, the rise and fall of the curtain; of separate spaces of actors and audience, or bridging those spaces; and turning on and off the houselights or the stagelights—all these things are intrinsic in the essence of a play, some people doing and other people watching. They must *never* be taken for granted and treated conventionally.

In principle, a different kind of play requires entirely remodeling the theatre architecture. The palace front, the apron, the proscenium, the round are different kinds of *plot*.

At present the Pirandellian lack-of-a-curtain, that indicates the ambiguity between what is real and what is appearance, has become an indiscriminate fad. It was inevitable. Advance-guard theatres, that indeed have a little more community reality than the audience, turn on the audience and say, "*You* are living in an illusion!" and so they omit the curtain.

But the curtain has nothing to do with illusion, but with watching. "Look! this is worth watching. Now don't look, go home."

When, at the end of *The Young Disciple*, the bawling boy falls and half tears down the curtain, I guess I mean to say that I do not find the state of things acceptable (finished), but that you are to go home anyway.

At the end of *Faustina*, however, the actress steps through the absent fourth wall into your space, no longer an actress, and then I don't know what would occur. In fact, the lady was an actress and refused to step out of the play, so the production fell to pieces. Well, that too is something that occurs.

VI

Acting is worth watching. Simply, that a person gestures and speaks according to some preconceived notion or formula, obedient to the unseen.

It is curious. If I notice such obedient, pre-planned, alienated behavior going on in a factory or army or where one person has fallen under another's influence, I find it abominable and I work to free the slaves. If I see a person repeating a neurotic compulsion or behaving in a rehearsed way rather than spontaneously, I am depressed. Yet if it is a parade, a dance routine or acting, either on stage or off, there is an intimation of something divine, as the folk in the Bible keep re-enacting God's plan.

My plays—*Jonah, Cain and Abel, The Family of Abraham* —are full of such ritualism; most likely this is why I retell Bible stories. In Noh plays the climax is nothing but a repetition of a past event. This is why I imitate them, and also because they finally become speechless.

Just so I find choral speaking astounding and I write it in whenever I get the chance. All speaking the same words! Yet when this very thing happens in politics or schooling, I am contemptuous.

When it's possible, I fall into regular meters—but I don't like to subject my characters to *my* rhythms, they must come to the meter themselves. It's madly exciting when in classical plays the half-verses of the angry actors unerringly fill out the trimeters. It is because they have rebelliously broken the trimeters that we know that they are angry and that *we* feel angry.

Alas! the fact that I find this kind of ritual repetition so fascinating must indicate some important characteristic of myself, probably psychotic. But it is a psychosis so regressed that there is no cure for it, in fallen man. Perhaps it is what it is to be an artist.

If the obedient ritual is man-imposed or compulsory, we must resist it at all costs. If it is free and playful, it is divine and thrilling, and for it we sacrifice our happiness in this world.

VII

At present they are downgrading speech on the stage, and this is justified to the extent that speech is "about" something rather than *is*. For whatever is on the stage must primarily be a presence, a force, an act. (Though, of course, discursive speech is a useful auxiliary to what is going on, like any other stage property.)

But speech *is* a presence, a force, an act. It is outcries and music; quarreling and persuasion; the characteristically human acts of reciting and narrating. Especially with poets it is hard to say what is the thing and what is "about" the thing. They seem to make a love poem in order to seduce, and then we find that they have fallen in love only to make the poem!

Miming is being exaggerated today. It diminishes force and presence to make people communicate like the deaf and dumb. But miming is powerful where people are *indeed* speechless—with rage, embarrassment, astonishment, deep peace.

I myself have been most concerned to study the relation of the specific act, speaking, with the other kinds of acts. The reader will find that the crucial theatrical problem in *Faustina* is: when can characters speak and when is it absurd or sick for them to speak? My coup, I think, is to make it plausible for the Gladiator to speak rationally even when he is helpless and about to have his throat cut. In *The Return from Moriah*, when Isaac is totally bawling because mama died, he also turns it off as one switches off a light, and asks interestedly, "Is this what people do?"

To my taste, it is a weakness in Shakespere that his people blab away *in extremis*, granting that it is sometimes splendid blabbing. One is almost reminded of the hilarious scene in *Medea* when, within, she is killing the screaming children and the Chorus outside keeps chattering, "Oh dear, something is amiss."

The best and, I think, complete study is in Noh: the narrative explanatory speech, the song as you go, the quarrel and persuasion speech, the gradual lyrical meters and expressive speech, incoherence, silence; reflectiveness and the return to our ordinary condition, including speech. Obviously it is this model that I am continually consulting in the dances in *The Young Disciple* and *Faustina* and in all my plays that have dances, and most of my plays have dances.

VIII

I make plays in a long tradition of men making plays. In my opinion, even if there were no such tradition, we would make plays. For instance, I see that at one year old my little daughter puts on shows for us to watch. But certainly I make my kind of plays because of Racine, Irish vaudeville, morality plays and Noh plays.

My disposition as a poet is not to innovate unless I have to. Simply, if Calderon, Goethe or Synge has hit on a style or scene that, with renovation, fits me, I like to wear the hand-me-down. It's economical—it's a way to organize a lot of experience—for nobody can organize big chunks of experience from scratch. There is an accumulative history of poetry just as of science. Those who are not learned, or scorn learning, merely borrow right and left in confusion.

On the other hand, if I need something unconventional for something new, I improvise it with a good conscience and no thought whatever of being unconventional.

No doubt I have a style of my own. Any poet who works a lot and with integrity will inevitably gradually accumulate his own vocabulary; modify to his purposes the devices that work for him; and even begin to streamline his own early manner. But I have very little awareness of what my style is, and critics have not bothered to tell me.

Frankly, I am at sea when they talk about "modern" or "contemporary." The authors who move me *all* seem to me to be contemporaries—they speak to me directly—though most of them are unfortunately dead. I fancy, too, that some of them approve of me.

But it is not with impunity that I write in the Western tradition as if it were alive. (It probably isn't, but I don't have any other.) For instance, during the thick of the Civil Rights struggle, a little group revived my *Hagar and Ishmael* at a church; but the critic of the *Village Voice* complained about their mounting such a musty old story.

Naturally, as a playwright slighted by the public, I make many spiteful and lonely remarks. But I would be less than candid if I did not say that when I am actually making a play or a poem, I am absorbed and have plenty of company.

IX

So! These are my cheerful remarks about the Art of the Theatre; and the fact is that I am fifty-three years old and I have no life in the theatre. *What* am I talking about?

When we talk about the *medium* of an art, we are like Adam in paradise, for the media of art are practical, like the materials to hand in paradise. Except in architecture, media are made of cheap stuff, mud and rock and noise and light and people moving and blabbing.

But when it comes to *practicing* an art, then we are engaged as we unfortunately *are*. The plays in this volume were written in 1941, 1948 and 1955, and I am writing this preface in 1964.

To me, writing for the theatre is the only kind of writing that is not lonely, and if I had my choice I would write mainly for the theatre. But I have not had the choice because the theatre has not been willing to have me.

To write for the theatre means to belong to a company for whose known actors I make appropriate speeches that ring beforehand in my ears; at whose rehearsals I swiftly tailor a scene so that they may all shine at their best. I do not have such a company. And the company does not have me.

And the audience and I have fallen into a ridiculous misunderstanding. The ordinary scenes I like are so ordinary that the ordinary audience couldn't care less. And on the other hand, if I use sentences that I think are very true, then they don't know what I'm batting about. I think that I am wrestling with an important problem of my country, and the audience is not aware that such a problem even exists.

Needless to say, the dilemma works in reverse. Most of their plays and all of their movies bore *me*. But I ought to have a better understanding with my neighbors in order to write plays for them.

Yet the audience is right, it is always right, for nobody has asked the playwright to come forward. *Are* the Americans right? It would be strange, since they are so wrong about everything else.

And suppose that *I* am "right"—what good does that do? A play is today and the audience is today.

X

My considered judgment is this:

Some of my hang-ups are only my own and there is no reason why other people should be interested. For instance, they have their psychosexual delusions and I have mine. That's too bad for me—I'm in the minority.

But there are other things I have to offer which, if I may say so, are too important and simple for present-day Americans to take seriously. And that's too bad for them as well as me. After a while—after I am good and dead—I stoically count on being a statue in the park.

Worse than either of these difficulties, however, is the

miserable *technical* dilemma of trying to say simply, in simple scenes, what probably requires considerable *prior* explanation; and especially to an audience that no longer carefully listens to plain English and that mistakes a glossy format for the art of the theatre. Then I myself fall into every kind of trap of bad theatre. Sometimes I explain too much. Sometimes I impatiently throw the audience the bone of a prosy little essay that kills theatre. Sometimes I forthrightly stay with my own perception and beautifully move myself, my friends and nobody else.

Let me make a comparison with the two living playwrights whom I esteem, Beckett and Genet. These artists deal powerfully with important matters that, it seems to me, *are* available to live Americans at present, for they deal with extremes. But I am out of touch just because I am engaged in a more middle ground; I have not given up on fatherhood, community, vocation, rational politics, benevolent nature, the culture of the Western world. I suppose there are two opposite reasons for my perseverance or delusion in these things: I think more soundly than those other playwrights, and I am too cowardly to risk as much as they do.

XI

It is in this unhappy plight that I make a pathetic pitch for community in all my books, and also in these plays. I refuse to concede that our community does not exist. Presumably, if it existed, it would solve my dilemma.

But I'm certainly not getting any younger.

PAUL GOODMAN

New York City
September, 1964

Contents

The Young Disciple

Martyrology in Three Acts

THE YOUNG DISCIPLE *was first produced by The Living Theatre, Judith Malina and Julian Beck, Directors, at The Living Theatre Studio, New York City, on October 12, 1955, with the following cast:*

(IN ORDER OF APPEARANCE)

WOMAN	Margery Hargrove/Diane Rhodes
OLD MAN	Henry Proach
YOUNG DISCIPLE	Hooper Dunbar
CASPAR	William Vines
MELCHIOR	Walter Mullen
BALTHASAR	Shirley Stoler
TOLERANT MAN	Ace King
CHILD	Sharon Stock
BOY	Mark William
OLD CRONE	Judith Malina
OUR MASTER	Philip Smith
FIRST SPOKESMAN	
SECOND SPOKESMAN	
THIRD SPOKESMAN	
FIRST OLD WOMAN, ERNESTINE	Katherine Lurker
SECOND OLD WOMAN, JESSIE	Jean Barr
THIRD OLD WOMAN	
FRIEND	
CROWD	

Directed and designed by JULIAN BECK

Assistant Director, SØREN AGENOUX

Music by PIERRE SCHAEFFER

ACT ONE

Scene One

As the curtain rises, an OLD MAN *and a* WOMAN *are on stage. At once the* YOUNG DISCIPLE *staggers on, backward. They stand dispersed in frozen attitudes, astonished. They are emitting astonished, indrawn gasps. The* OLD MAN *keeps gasping, even while the others speak, making high sounds like the indrawn breaths of a harmonica player. Later he also breathes heavily out, groaning.*

WOMAN (*Low in pitch and not too loud*)   I can't believe my eyes.

YOUNG DISCIPLE (*In fear*)   Did you—did you—did you see it?
> (*They support the* OLD MAN, *who seems to be in pain with his heavy breathing. They are clinging to one another for support*)

ALL THREE (*Finally*)   Eyes—we can't—can't believe our eyes.

OLD MAN (*As if awakening, draws away from them*)   What happened? Where am I?

YOUNG DISCIPLE (*With a shriek that must tingle the spine of the audience*)   Aiiiiiii! I am going blind! (*Staggering blindly about, reaching with his hands*) Which way? Blind! I never saw enough day, now it's too late. Which way—which way is it? (*Whimpering*) Aiii. Tell me which way is it.

3

(*Enter from the right the Three Wise Ones,* CASPAR, MELCHIOR *and* BALTHASAR, *dressed in the three primary colors. At once* CASPAR *walks over to the staggerer and shakes him by the shoulders*)

CASPAR Stop it, boy. Snap out of it. Stop it, I say. Here, what's this? (*He shakes his fist in front of his eyes*) Smell it!

YOUNG DISCIPLE That's a fist. Owww. (*Crying*) Don't hit me. I don't know you. I never did you any harm.

CASPAR Nobody intends to hit you. *Open* your eyes. No, keep them open. You're not blind at all. Nobody can see if he keeps his eyes shut. You're a grown boy, you know *that.*

YOUNG DISCIPLE Yes . . .

CASPAR *Keep* them open.

YOUNG DISCIPLE Yes. I can see. It is day.

OLD MAN What happened?

WOMAN Where are we?

MELCHIOR Our Master demonstrates the case. In his person he shows nothing but what is the case. Naturally you can't believe your eyes. It is the same with us. But what do we do? We blink. Stop staring. We do not stare. Stop holding your breath. We do not hold our breath. Then we simply move and do something, whatever is called for. Mostly we don't talk about it.

YOUNG DISCIPLE What did you say?

4

MELCHIOR (*Dryly*) Mostly, I said, we don't talk about it.
That's important. Not another word.
(*Frustrated pause*)

BALTHASAR (*To the rescue*) I like this. The young man
says it is day, so it is:

The day is clear as day
and March like the start of spring,
everywhere the sky
spreads further than the earth!

The clouds are shapes of vapor
in the high atmosphere;
sunlight pours from the sun;
the heat of it is warm.

CASPAR *and* MELCHIOR
Everywhere the sky
is spread further than the earth.
Heat is warm!

BALTHASAR The past day was,
it is written down in words—

YOUNG DISCIPLE (*Indignantly*) What rubbish! March *is*
the start of spring. "The clouds are shapes of vapor in the
high atmosphere"—of course they are, what else do you
think clouds are? Is that news? Is that supposed to be
poetry?

MELCHIOR You have hit it! You have hit it! Follow us!

CASPAR (*Taking him by the sleeve*) Please, not so fast.
This one tends to go blind, he is in love with the day.

5

MELCHIOR   No matter. Everybody has something. I am in love with Adam and I am subject to fits of hatred and contempt for these persons.

CASPAR (*To* YOUNG DISCIPLE)   Do you hear? You are to come along with us.

YOUNG DISCIPLE (*Abashed, after a momentary silence*)   Let me pray. (*He falls to his knees*)

> Day, save me! I have been entranced
> by the eternal forms.
> By love and death are they strong,
> a process of two steps.
>
> By love they came to be
> and by death they are.
> O unpeople me, my day
> my only one, this place
>
> of sorcery where I lie
> —and let only surprise
> surprise and falling asleep
> surprise and sleep be my gait
>
> surprise as when forth cast
> from the finger of God the Man
> looked back at him with boundlessly
> boundlessly open eyes.

BALTHASAR (*Touching him*)   Come, son, you have prayed enough to your idol. Let us go.

YOUNG DISCIPLE   Which way is it that we must go?

(*Exeunt the Three Wise Ones followed by the* YOUNG DISCIPLE)

OLD MAN (*Flatly*)   What happened?

WOMAN (*Flatly*)   I can't believe my eyes.

OLD MAN (*Flatly*)   Which way is it that we must go?

WOMAN (*Flatly*)   No, where *are* we?

OLD MAN   Everywhere the sky spreads further than the earth.

WOMAN   That past day was, it is written down in words.

Curtain

The curtain rises on a street. The Three Wise Ones, front left center. To the right rear are three or four of the CROWD, *and the* YOUNG DISCIPLE.

CASPAR Why does he have to come back here to his home town? Our Master has fallen among these home folks the way a man has an accident, and he's walking with a limp.

MELCHIOR A prophet has no honor among his own people.

CASPAR (*Sharply*) That's because he's stupid among his own people. As soon as he arrived here he began to speak with a stammer. People look at him with eyes that knew him as a child and so he becomes a child. A hayseed! From the country! From up in the mountains where a stream runs.

BALTHASAR He says that he has come back here in order to have a good fuck.

CASPAR Who is he going to fuck with here? It's not his mother, I can tell you that. She's dead. Too late! Too late! Too late!
     (*The crowd bursts out laughing and begins to jeer*)

MELCHIOR Pay them no mind; they take it out on us because we are princes. (*Proudly*) We are princes by habit and use and from far countries! We know what rank is—it is nothing to us—and so we can tolerate it, and breathe hard, and begin to hope insanely when suddenly we have met one of the angels. We saw him take wing and we flushed, and we cried out—

BALTHASAR   We cried out, "I can't believe my eyes!"

MELCHIOR   But these people—
   (*The* YOUNG DISCIPLE *crosses over to them*)

CROWD
   Fake! Fake! Fake!
   Dupes!
   It's the son of a tailor!
   The princes are using him!
   Half o' them are Jews, the other half are goyim!

MELCHIOR   (*To* YOUNG DISCIPLE)   What are they saying?

YOUNG DISCIPLE   What do you think? They are impressing
   on me that I don't understand chicanery and such other
   homely motives. It is after all only the son of so-and-so
   on the next street. Or contrariwise: he doesn't have any
   ax to grind; what are we peddling? Where's there a buck
   in it? Nothing! Also, when he walks along the road, he
   doesn't cast a shadow.

CASPAR   *Did* they dare to say that! (*He seizes a man of the
   crowd by the neck*) Damn you, you liars! Sin against the
   flesh—it shall not be forgiven you, to say that my master
   has no substance and does not cast a shadow! This you
   never saw with your own eyes! Nay, as he walks by in the
   sun, my master cast a shadow of deepest blue, like an old
   and perfect apple tree I used to lie under, and that also
   has not ceased to bear fruit. Is this flesh that *you* have?
   (*He pinches him and the man cringes, but* MELCHIOR
   restrains him)

MELCHIOR   Let be. These folk are not yet fearful of their
   sanity—what can they do but jeer? They are embarrassed

9

by the feelings rising in them, like an amorous girl who feels tickled and giggles. Soon she is beside herself. They are still taking refuge in ridicule. Listen to this one—

(*An* OLD CRONE *enters hobbling, crying out plaintively*)

OLD CRONE   A sign! A sign! Why doesn't he give us a sign and prove himself? Give us a sign! We want to believe! A sign.

MELCHIOR   Isn't it pitiful? Old lady, what kind of sign do you expect? Your longing is the same as everyone's, but you want to be surprised in some way that you expect. Don't you understand that you cannot be surprised in that way? Now here he is.

(*Enter* OUR MASTER, *limping. He is more real than the others, as if, let us say, they are wearing grease paint, he not. He must be remarkable neither for beauty nor bearing nor personality; but he has a concentrated presence. As he appears to her, the* OLD CRONE *gasps with astonishment.* OUR MASTER *supports her*)

OUR MASTER   What is it, old mother?

OLD CRONE   It is what he said: "Now here he is." Here now you are. This is beyond belief.

(*She sits down and weeps*)

OUR MASTER (*As he is speaking, a kid of the crowd creeps up behind him, concealing something behind his back*) It is true, I feel powerless here. I doubt that I am powerless, but that is neither here nor there. How would I know until I come to act? I feel like the adolescent who comes to his first fuck and can't get a hard-on.

(*With a wild laugh the kid crowns him with a mushy watermelon. The* CROWD *derisively pelts them all with rotten eggs, soft tomatoes and garbage*)

CROWD

    Filth!

    Fake!

    Cockless creatures!

    Garbage!

    Hyannn! Hyannn!

CASPAR (*Who has grabbed the kid and a man in either hand*) What shall I do? Shall I brain them together or separately?

MELCHIOR Let be, let be. They are children. Just walk out of it.

    (*The Three Wise Ones and the* YOUNG DISCIPLE *begin to walk off with dignity. Suddenly* OUR MASTER *is convulsed with laughter*)

OUR MASTER (*Roaring with laughter*) The way you look! The way you look!

    (*He himself hits them with a tomato. Now all five are convulsed with laughter. They roar helplessly and lean against one another for support. The* BOY *laughs with them, capering about and clapping his hands*)

MELCHIOR (*Wiping the tears from his eyes*) Really, really! I never learned these country customs.

CASPAR But, oh! they are like tonic wine. More! More!

    (*As they laugh the* CROWD *cowers. Exeunt* OUR MASTER *and the* BOY, *joyful*)

BALTHASAR (*To the* CROWD) You consummate asses!

YOUNG DISCIPLE   That's right, dear, you harangue them. Wait, I'll get you a box.

>   (*He helps her up on a box*)

BALTHASAR   (*Like Emma Goldman*)   Tell me, I'm curious. What advantage is it to destroy your prophets? What they say will come to pass anyway.

CROWD   (*Muttering*)   What they *say!* Owww, the things *they* say!

FIRST SPOKESMAN   There's plenty of advantage!

SECOND SPOKESMAN   Yes, plenty!

BALTHASAR   Well, what is it? Speak up, you in the back.

FIRST SPOKESMAN   For instance, if we kill 'em before the disaster happens, then we can feel guilty about it afterwards. It was all *my* fault. *We* did it.

SECOND SPOKESMAN   Yes, kill 'em. Hurray for us!

FIRST SPOKESMAN   That saves our feelings.

SECOND SPOKESMAN AND OTHERS   Ee-yow! Kill 'em! Hurray for me!

>   (*The* CROWD *begins to recover and advances*)

THIRD SPOKESMAN   *You're* what causes all the trouble!

FIRST SPOKESMAN   Yah! There he lies, dead as a mouse; the old fool couldn't save even himself!

SECOND SPOKESMAN   Kill 'em all!

FIRST SPOKESMAN   *He* never had the secret of saving, why is he dishing it out?

THIRD SPOKESMAN   He can dish it out but he can't take it!

FIRST SPOKESMAN Is it our fault we're in trouble? What could *we* do? It was unpredictable!

BALTHASAR Unpredictable? I *beg* your pardon, you surprise me. He *did* predict it, that's just what he predicted.

FIRST SPOKESMAN He? Who?

THIRD SPOKESMAN What he? Where is he?

SECOND SPOKESMAN Let me at 'im, let me at 'im! Here, hold my coat.

FIRST SPOKESMAN Never heard of such a person. To what are you referring?

THIRD SPOKESMAN We'll teach *him* to butt in!

ALL Yah! yah! yah! yah! yah!

FIRST SPOKESMAN We can do without these second-guessers!

ALL Yah! Yah! Hurrah for us!
(*Exeunt congratulating themselves*)

BALTHASAR (*Fanning the air and descending heavily from the box*) I'm at a loss.
"He? Who? What he? There the old fool lies dead—"
They'll do it, too! "Never heard of such a person!"

CASPAR Let me at 'im! (*Howls with joy*) Except that they'll do it, they'll do it! But I can't help myself. They'll kill him, too.
(*He howls with merriment*)

MELCHIOR No question about it, the people have more soul than we cultivated ones. They have infected us with their hilarity, whether we will or no. It's simply a matter of available soul, and they have it. They can, in an instant,

13

form into one, and they form us into their one; we speak of the people—and they will kill Our Master—and we too are the people.

YOUNG DISCIPLE   Yes, it's quiet and lonely here without their foolishness, like an empty tavern.

CASPAR   They must have soul-power because my knees are weak. Frankly, the tears are rolling down my cheeks.

BALTHASAR (*Soberly*)   Yes, they have power. They can project into empty space their deepest unfelt wishes, they can call into being nonexistent monsters that are soon perceived by every eye. Surely the people have a power of soul.

Curtain

The curtain rises. The Two Wise Men are gathering shadows of OUR MASTER *from the ground.*

CASPAR   This one's a beauty. Shall I try to take it? It's too elaborate, it will break into pieces.

MELCHIOR   Let me see. (*In admiration*) God! Definite, unmistakable, portentous. What do you suppose it is? (*Assuming various postures, he tries to cast the shadow*) It is elaborate. Oh! Look. The sun was over there and this is when he doubled up laughing at you and me, and then that young hoodlum began to laugh and broke through the hedge into the garden. Leave it, leave it, it will break.

CASPAR   (*Roving about*)   Look at these. I've got to have one of these. Limping. Always limping. And suddenly here he startles you, leaping ahead for a mile. Here. This is a good practical shape that illustrates the whole series: limping. Our Master at home. (*He goes to work to pick up the shadow, and holds it up*) This one I'll take back with me to the north, and what shall I tell them? How shall I put it—what do you think?

MELCHIOR   (*Reflecting*)   The weakness of Our Master— when he felt powerless—was like the blow of the tired lion, that crushes you to death. But you don't die. People are tough.

CASPAR   Hmm. And here?
    (*Again the other imitates the posture*)

MELCHIOR   Shadow animals for the little girl. That's the wolf. That's the dragon, with smoke rings. (*Simply*) See,

my shadows do not stay, but his stay. Let me take up one
of these little wolves.

(*Enter the* YOUNG DISCIPLE)

YOUNG DISCIPLE   What are you two doing?

CASPAR   We are looking over the shadows of Our Master.
Haven't you ever done that?

YOUNG DISCIPLE   What, do you *keep* them? But they are
shadows. I'm sure he would hate that.

CASPAR   Don't embarrass us, young man. You're a native of
this region. We come from far off. We collect souvenirs.

MELCHIOR   It's nothing to be ashamed of. Wait, let me
show you something quite perfect. It's my prize. I don't
think I have ever shown it to anybody. (*He searches in
his wallet*) You'll see—it's only a little head. There!

CASPAR (*Astonished*)   In the name of the holy spirit!

YOUNG DISCIPLE   Oh! What is it?
(*He begins to tremble*)

MELCHIOR (*To* CASPAR)   Don't *you* recognize it?

CASPAR   Don't I recognize it! What do you take me for? Of
course I recognize it. It is from the Marriage, when he
spoke softly to the two who loved each other and he
showed that it was not impossible, it was not impossible—
it was not even difficult—for two who loved each other to
want each other to be happy.

YOUNG DISCIPLE (*Impulsively*)   I don't believe it! (*Abashed*)
I can't believe my ears—what you say— (*He falls silent,
trembles more violently. Faltering*) Tell me—what is it?
What does it mean, that these shadows persist?

16

MELCHIOR   The meaning of dreams in this magic day is clear as they befall, without the need or use to think it out. Where the shadows fall, they lie.

YOUNG DISCIPLE (*Thickly*)   Yes, that is what it means.

CASPAR   Are you aware that you are trembling?

YOUNG DISCIPLE (*Abashed*)   No. I was not aware of it till now.

CASPAR   Practice being more aware.
(*Exeunt duo. The* YOUNG DISCIPLE *clutches at his eyes, blind, and for a moment he staggers as in the first scene, but silent. Then he opens his eyes and there is a pause. He says*)

YOUNG DISCIPLE

Such ordinary joy as is the day
when once we dare to stand out o' the way—
(*He begins to tremble again, with weak knees. But now he gives in to it, and the trembling spreads. He trembles violently, standing mid-stage, for perhaps two minutes, also breathing finally very regularly. And he says*)

Such ordinary joy as is the day
when once we dare to stand out o' the way
I felt; my hunger did not sicken to
disappointment nor my misery
darken the day with spite. I yawned and grew
heavy and fell into this reverie.
(*He yawns*)

Swift Curtain

ACT TWO

Scene One

FIRST *and* SECOND OLD WOMEN *are on stage. Their dialogue is half gossiping, half telling beads. The pace is scherzando and accelerando.*

FIRST OLD WOMAN   Do you know what he did?

SECOND OLD WOMAN   No, what?

FIRST OLD WOMAN   He went across the water!

SECOND OLD WOMAN   I'm not surprised. I'm not a bit surprised.

FIIRST OLD WOMAN.   I *saw* him cross the water.

SECOND OLD WOMAN   I'm not a bit surprised at *what* he'll do.

FIRST OLD WOMAN   I saw it with my own eyes.

SECOND OLD WOMAN   *Did* you? Lordy, Lordy, he crossed the water.

FIRST OLD WOMAN   That's *right!* But do you know what that Mrs. Atsageooris said? She says, "I don't believe it!" Hah, hah.

SECOND OLD WOMAN   Does she?

FIRST OLD WOMAN   So I says to her, "Hazel! Hazel!" I says, "I *saw* it! Do you mean to tell me you can sit there—" I says to her. "Hazel! Are you by any chance calling me a liar?" With my own eyes, with my own eyes. *Mrs.* Atsageooris!

SECOND OLD WOMAN   Is that what she said? Well, I like that. *I'm* not surprised. He went across the water.

FIRST OLD WOMAN   So then she says—so I says, "Hazel! Stop right there—there are *some* things—"
>   (*Enter left* BALTHASAR *and the* YOUNG DISCIPLE. *Enter right the* THIRD OLD WOMAN)

THIRD OLD WOMAN   He raised up the butcher's daughter!

FIRST OLD WOMAN   Yes! She was dead as a mouse!

THIRD OLD WOMAN   Right in the little room over the pawn-shop.

SECOND OLD WOMAN (*Gasping in breath*)   Ohhh, Ohhh. He went across the water! He went across the water! I saw him cross the water.
>   (*The sentences are her way of getting out her in-drawn breath*)

FIRST OLD WOMAN   So I says, "Hazel! stop right there!"

THIRD OLD WOMAN   Is that what he did? Well, I am not surprised!

FIRST OLD WOMAN (*To* THIRD)   Do you know what *she* said?
>   (*So they continue, quieter, in the background, faster and faster. It is punctuated by "Hazel!" "Right in the little room over the pawnshop," and the gasping in-breath*)

YOUNG DISCIPLE   What the devil are they doing?

BALTHASAR   Why, that's pure confabulation, to fill up a blank space in experience. They have to say *something*.

Almost nobody can leave it blank. You're new. You'll see a lot of it.

YOUNG DISCIPLE (Angry)   What in hell difference does it make to them whether or not he crossed the water? So we did, in a boat.

BALTHASAR Please. What difference does it make to *you* that they say it? Why are you so disturbed? Listen—

OLD WOMEN (In the background, a trifle louder for fifteen seconds)
    So I says to Hazel, "Stop right there . . ."
    Oh, she was dead, all right, dead as a mouse . . .
    Well, I'm not surprised, I'm not a *bit* surprised . . .
    Mrs. Atsageooris!
    Right in the little room over the pawnshop . . .
    There you are, some people . . .

BALTHASAR Just listen. It's fascinating. Aren't you interested in such things? They keep saying I see I see and their eyes aren't seeing anything at all. They recount marvels and their voices are toneless. It's always the same banal anecdote. They don't have the vitality to embroider it. They are beside themselves with surprise and so they say I'm not surprised, I'm not a bit surprised. Underneath they are obsessively telling beads to ward off a nameless excitement, but they turn it into sociable gossip in order to live on a little. This is a beautiful human invention. Why are *you* so exasperated?

YOUNG DISCIPLE I'm exasperated because I'm getting sick. I'm going to vomit.

OLD WOMEN (*Loud chorus*)
Lórdy, lórdy, seóolie kóoris
ínkoménie dópsi óoris
felláir immáne bósti déllo
ísskini bár feróoshióli

BALTHASAR Now they are theologizing, and the golden
lotuses snake up from the noisome mud and open broad.
I am astonished. Wonder at it! The lovely Asclepiadic
rhythm coming from the lips of these unlettered peasants!
Would you predict that poetry would come out of such
nonsense?
(*Beside himself, the* YOUNG DISCIPLE *rushes at them
and takes the middle woman by the shoulders and
shakes her*)

YOUNG DISCIPLE You old bitch. Stop right there! What *are*
you maundering about? You came to your senses for one
instant in your life and you couldn't believe your eyes.
Hang *onto* that instant! Keep it! Stay with it! Why don't
you say, "I don't know! I don't know! I don't know!"

SECOND OLD WOMAN (*Whining*) But he did cross the
water. I saw him. I did see him. With my own eyes, with
my own eyes.

FIRST OLD WOMAN Yes, and I said to Mrs. Atsageooris,
"Hazel—"

THIRD OLD WOMAN She was dead as a mouse!

YOUNG DISCIPLE (*In fury*) You're driving me crazy. (*Intensely*) Rather than permit something new to occur in
your wretched existences, something that might make a
difference, you are willing to betray our beautiful sensible

21

world that has in it the field and the stars and the sea with its horizon. You are willing to deny the existence of the dark night— (*He bursts into tears*) You would imagine that you had reason to be attached to the way in which we live.

(*He becomes sick and vomits*)

FIRST OLD WOMAN (*Shrieks*) Aiiiiii! Aiiiiii!

SECOND OLD WOMAN (*Shrieks*) Aiiiiiiiiiiii!

THIRD OLD WOMAN (*Suddenly*) I can fly!
(*She falls in a faint. There is a pause. The* FIRST *and* SECOND OLD WOMEN *come to her aid and they say tenderly and with great dignity*)

FIRST *and* SECOND OLD WOMEN
Are you happy, my sister, are you in the best of health?
Nobody can be spared, *you* are necessary to *me*.
Come back! Only a god can linger by himself,
so much the worse for him! Let him be.
Our sister has rode off on the back of a white bull
that browsed on the flowers and plunged into the deep,
the promise of ages in order to fulfill.
Come back, sister, out of your black sleep.
(*The fainted woman revives and sits up. They painfully and silently support her off, while the* YOUNG DISCIPLE *looks on amazed*)

BALTHASAR (*Confronting him*) Young man, you are rude.
(*Exit. The* YOUNG DISCIPLE *stands a moment alone. The* TOLERANT MAN *enters*)

TOLERANT MAN   Young man, I saw that. You were terribly harsh with those old ladies; you fail to take the circumstances into account. Let me speak to you as a friend. These are extraordinary times and there are extraordinary events. As for me, I don't know whether or not he crossed the water, as they say, whatever that means. Also I don't care. But there is *something* extraordinary here. Why do you scoff at their poor literal statement, like a village atheist?

YOUNG DISCIPLE   (*Clasping and unclasping his fists*)   It needed only this! It needed only this benevolent tolerance —to call me an atheist. I am at a loss. Here is the truth— Here is the truth and made fit for pigs! You lying pig! (*He grabs the* TOLERANT MAN *by the lapels and looks him earnestly in the face. Suddenly he is pounding him across the shoulders with a stick*) You *pig!* You *pig!*

TOLERANT MAN   (*With fear and offended dignity*)   Don't. Don't. Let me alone. Are you demented?

YOUNG DISCIPLE   (*Shouting, shouting*)   Not *extra*ordinary! Not *extra*ordinary! *But usual, usual!* Can't you tell the difference, you pig? *This* is extraordinary, what you are feeling now. *Feel* it! (*One last blow. Then he again holds him by the lapels and looks at him earnestly*) Can't you see, man, that by your understanding half-truths you make it impossible for me to exist? I cannot exist in the extraordinary; I cannot live in extreme situations. I have to live on from hour to hour and from day to day. As usual. As usual. I cannot rely on the extraordinary. (*He lets go. The* TOLERANT MAN *sits on the ground cowering, while the* YOUNG DISCIPLE *stands over* *him with a stick*) *Whom* are you reproaching with your charge of atheism? We are the fellowship of paradise, we who have dared to draw near, to live near, the dangerous edge of a fact. We have pursued it from the ends of the earth. He did not come to us! No— (*Enter* OUR MASTER, *quietly*) Here you are. (*The stick falls from his hand*) You are angry.

OUR MASTER I have no sign to give. With what shall I prove what? I give only itself, as the creator strews the day with a *large* hand.

YOUNG DISCIPLE No! What you give is your angry face.
(*The* TOLERANT MAN *picks himself up and flees, crying*)

TOLERANT MAN Help!

YOUNG DISCIPLE (*Angry*) *He* can cry out in terror and flee. I can't afford this luxury. They have nine lives like cats, but I am throwing away my only life. (OUR MASTER *stands before him with the expression on his face changing rapidly*) What are you thinking of? Your face keeps changing. I look at your face and moment by moment it is dartingly reflecting the conjunction of my stars. I am projecting. You are looking at me sadly.

OUR MASTER (*Expressing no emotion*) Are you afraid of me too?

YOUNG DISCIPLE Please do not ask me this. For when you ask it, and because you ask it, a stab of fear has stabbed me in the breast under the throat. (OUR MASTER *makes as if to leave him*) No! Listen to me! (*Takes him by the arm*) We were out in the boat and there was a storm. It was a fearful storm but we were not afraid, for it was a storm. But you said, "Don't be afraid of the storm"; you said, "It is a storm." And the water began to be calm. Don't you see? It is *you* we were afraid of, when you made it calm for us.

OUR MASTER   I understand you.

YOUNG DISCIPLE (*Outcry*)   My present moment has me by the throat.

OUR MASTER (*Enthusiastic*)   Good! Stay with that close! You won't choke. Risk it.
    (*He walks away, leaving him*)

(*Quick curtain*)

In front of the curtain. MELCHIOR is instructing the BOY in making a fire with a burning glass, concentrating the beam on a ball of paper. From the left falls a very hot spot on them, the Sun, and this they are catching in the glass. The action follows the poem.

MELCHIOR   His eye—

> His eye is a burning glass,
> does in the heart of tinder place
> a real image of the sun
> trembling bright and alone,
> a mighty seed of fire
> is entombed there.
>
> A curl of smoke means nothing, but
> when smoke begins to pour and vomit
> look, with a puff as if
> blowing itself alive,
> flames are crazy with freedom
> which is the prize of wisdom.

(*The paper flares up and they watch it burn out*) Do it yourself.

(*The BOY crumples up a ball of paper and repeats the operation*)

BOY   A *real* image of the sun—yes, it is hot. Trembling bright—alone. There is the smoke. A little smoke means nothing. But when smoke begins to pour and vomit! (*The fire burns*) Yes.

(*MELCHIOR goes apart a little and kneels to pray*)

MELCHIOR

       I make my god man-like, nor fear
       to be an idol's fool, for
          so hard I think of man the thought
          has crumbled into absolute
       un-Nature! Oh! and he will save
       me in the little work and love
          I lust in day by day until
          my name he elects to call.
       (*They go off*)

The curtain rises on a poor room. The THIRD OLD WOMAN *is out of her wits, lying on a pallet.* FIRST OLD WOMAN *is standing looking at her.* SECOND OLD WOMAN *on one of two rockers sewing. Between the rockers a demijohn.*

FIRST OLD WOMAN (*At the bedside*) She's not asleep. Her eyes are open.
  (*She sits, they sew and sigh*)

THIRD OLD WOMAN (*Weirdly, mechanically, not in her own voice*) Jo-el! Put that cat out! Out! (*Indistinguishable mumbling*) Dz dzh frr gh bld. Put him out and lock the door! Quick! Quick! Oooo, he's getting away.

FIRST OLD WOMAN She's cracked. (*Mimicking*) Jo-el! That's her old lady's voice, I remember it just like I'm sitting here. Joel was the oldest boy. He's dead too.

SECOND OLD WOMAN Poor dearie.

THIRD OLD WOMAN (*Prowling*) He got away! He got away! He's under the sofy! Jo-el! Quick quick. Quick and the dead. Tick tock tick tock.

FIRST OLD WOMAN The cat's out o' the bag at last. All her life—all her life she saw to it. She makes perfect sense. She makes perfect sense but you can't reach her.

SECOND OLD WOMAN No. There's no use. What do you say to a little comfort? (*She fills two cups from the demijohn and they drink. Earnestly*) It's wonderful what you *are* doing, to take her in this way, the shit and all. Not even a relative. Really, it's—touching.
  (*She is embarrassed*)

FIRST OLD WOMAN (*Simply*) And what about you?
    (*There is an embarrassed silence*)

SECOND OLD WOMAN Well, there it is. So what? I wouldn't
    expect it for myself. Ernestine, if I ever—I mean, not like
    that, but if I— (*Brutally, to cover her feelings*) Just tell
    them to throw me in the garbage.

THIRD OLD WOMAN (*Wildly*) The broom! The broom! Get
    the broom! Dz gll frm xxst mldtmemnbaeu nmbbb.
    (*And so on for fifteen seconds. Silence*)

FIRST OLD WOMAN She ain't human. You can't reach her.
    (*The other brings her chair close and says earnestly*)

SECOND OLD WOMAN Do you know, that's funny you should
    say that, you took the words right out o' my mouth. (*Em-
    barrassed*) Now don't you look at me queer. I been think-
    ing. I never had such thoughts in my life. I've got *ideas*!
    Now don't you look at me.

FIRST OLD WOMAN Oh come on, dearie, I wouldn't look at
    you queer. What's there to be ashamed of?
    (*The other pours another drink, a bracer*)

SECOND OLD WOMAN Well, don't you look at me queer.
    (*Plunging*) I mean—how do you know it's a human being,
    that's what I wonder. Now there you go, looking at me
    queer. I never had such thoughts in my life.

FIRST OLD WOMAN I'm not! I know *just* what you mean.
    How do you *know* it's a human being?

SECOND OLD WOMAN (*Rapidly*) How can you *tell*? I mean—
    supposing you're walking down the street and there it is.
    It looks like a man. But it might be a clothing dummy.
    (*Triumphant*)

FIRST OLD WOMAN *That* don't even move.

SECOND OLD WOMAN No, but you can't *reach* 'im! That's what I think. *She* (*Thumb*) can move, but she ain't human. Really, I never had such thoughts in my life, don't you look at me queer.

THIRD OLD WOMAN (*Nearer to her own voice*) Look out, baby, that cat's wild, he'll scratch.

FIRST OLD WOMAN (*Meditative*) You're absolutely right. We see eye to eye, you and I. It don't even need to *look* like a man, and still it's human, if you can reach it. Take a dog—a dog's human—but it ain't human *enough*. What about a talking dog; if she walks up to you and asks you for the time o' day. "Woof! woof! Madam, could you please tell me the time?" Is that a human being?

SECOND OLD WOMAN (*Positively*) Yes.

FIRST OLD WOMAN Yes, I agree too.
(*They pour another drink, on their agreement*)

SECOND OLD WOMAN (*Waving her cup*) I can prove it. Because what do *you* do? You try to be polite, you hide your face so the poor bitch can't see you smiling; you can't help smiling. Right?

FIRST OLD WOMAN Right! You can reach her.
(*They drink*)

THIRD OLD WOMAN *Heeeeeere* kitty kitty kitty kitty kitty kitty *hee eere* kitty kitty kitty . . . *heeere* kitty kitty.

SECOND OLD WOMAN O.K. That's settled *She* ain't human and a clothing dummy ain't human, an' a talking dog *is* human. Now what about one o' these machines?

FIRST OLD WOMAN Machines?

SECOND OLD WOMAN They say they got a machine that plays checkers. So *you* move, then *he* moves, then *you* move, then *he* moves, then *you* move, then *he* moves—

FIRST OLD WOMAN Yeah—yeah—

SECOND OLD WOMAN According to how *you* move. *He* moves according to how you move. But it's all wheels inside— brrr! whzz! bzz! move! Is that human?

FIRST OLD WOMAN You mean it's all wheels? Does it win?

SECOND OLD WOMAN Sometimes he wins, sometimes he loses. But is he *human*? It answers you, don't he? *You* move, then *he* moves. You can *reach* him. But what I want to know (*Demanding down-tapping finger*) —what I want to know, is it *human*? Is it a *man*? He's just wheels. Brrr, prrrr, bzzzz.

FIRST OLD WOMAN Can he talk?

SECOND OLD WOMAN Sure it can talk! What do you think? That's just wheels too. Prrr, bzzzzz, whah! "Hello? what number do you want? When you hear the signal, the time will be eleven thirty-seven. And how are you this rainy day?" Well?

FIRST OLD WOMAN (*Puzzled*) I dunno. If it can talk and he answers you back. (*Positively*) I dunno.

SECOND OLD WOMAN Good! Neither do I! We click.
(*They pour out another and drink*)

FIRST OLD WOMAN (*Suddenly rising and breathing heavily and staring in the other's face*) Jessie—!

SECOND OLD WOMAN Now, there you go. I knew it. Lookin' at me queer—

31

FIRST OLD WOMAN   No. (*Stage whisper*) What if it's got no body? You're walkin' down the street and all of a sudden it begins to talk to you out o' nowhere. It's a—a *presence*. (*Hoarse stage whisper*) It doesn't have a body.

SECOND OLD WOMAN (*Sigh of relief*) Phoo. You scared me. No. Definitely. Positively. That ain't a man. That's a ghost an' the hell with it.

THIRD OLD WOMAN   Miaoooouww, miauoooouww. *Heeeeere* kitty kitty kitty kitty. (*Child's whisper*) Where is he? He's in the outhouse. Heeeeere kitty kitty kitty.

FIRST OLD WOMAN (*Sitting down; simply*)   What about *him*?

SECOND OLD WOMAN   Him?

FIRST OLD WOMAN   Is *he* human?

SECOND OLD WOMAN   Yes. He's—tangible.
(*She giggles*)

FIRST OLD WOMAN   Tangible?
(*She giggles*)

SECOND OLD WOMAN   Yes, that's what he is. He's tangible. (*They giggle. They can't stop. They giggle in little trills, as in the third section of the "Grand Fugue"*) People say he don't cast a shadow, but it's not true. It ain't true. He casts a shadow. He's tangible. He's human.

FIRST OLD WOMAN   She ain't human, she's a god, she's an everlasting cat.

SECOND OLD WOMAN   He's human. He's a mortal man.
(*They giggle in little trills*)

Curtain

Scene Four

Before the curtain. TOLERANT MAN *and* FRIEND *enter from left. There is a wooden hydrant.*

TOLERANT MAN   What am *I* offended at? No! I'm not offended at getting a beating. I been knocked down before. I have learned to take it whence it comes, and the world is full o' people who should have their heads examined.

FRIEND   Then what?

TOLERANT MAN   Their fuckin' *secrecy*. Shh! shh! Who do they take themselves for? "We don't discuss that." "Generally we don't talk about it." (*Mimicking, he puts his finger to his lips and gives a silly smile. Then he vibrates his lips with his fingers like a maniac*) For God's sake, come off it! What do you think we are, children? . . . I ask about their program, about their credentials, anything; anything! He looks at me like a Chinaman and—listen to this (*Mimics*): "We do not mention supernatural beings." Mention! Really! Really!
　　(*Suddenly he is struck dumb. The other waits*)

FRIEND   Well? (*No answer*) Now what's the matter? (*No answer*) What's the matter with *you*? Lose your tongue? (*He shakes him*) (TOLERANT MAN *shakes his head and waves him away. He isn't talking*) Where *are* you, anyway? (*No answer*) Well, for Chrissake, if this ain't the limit! Now *I'm* offended. Fuck yourself.
　　(*Exit right.* TOLERANT MAN *goes through the curtain. Enter a Dog*)

DOG   (*Examining the hydrant*)   What's this for? (*He nib-*

bles) You can't eat it . . . (*He mounts*) And you can't fuck it.

Piss on it!
    (*He does and trots off*)

Scene Five

The curtain rises on the street. A rope is stretched a few inches above the ground. The street feels deserted. Enter the Three Wise Ones, the YOUNG DISCIPLE, *the* BOY.

BOY   It's too quiet. Where is everybody?

YOUNG DISCIPLE   They are lying in wait.

BOY   What are they waiting for? 1331562

YOUNG DISCIPLE   They are bracing themselves against some deadly danger they can dream up. They're waiting. They haven't thought of it yet. It will be quiet till something occurs to them to be afraid of.
   (BALTHASAR *feels the walls with her hands*)

BALTHASAR   (*Showing her hand*)   The walls are in a cold sweat. The street is trembling. The doorway has a dry throat. I have a dry throat.
   (*A stone comes whistling through the air and hits the wall*)

YOUNG DISCIPLE   It has occurred to them what to be afraid of! Us!
   (*Another stone*)

BOY   They have lousy aim but I don't like it!
   (*He ducks into hiding in a doorway*)

YOUNG DISCIPLE   He is right to run away, we are wrong to stand here. Why are we standing here? Where is Our Master?

BALTHASAR   He is in the woods hunting.

YOUNG DISCIPLE   Why am *I here?*

CASPAR   I'm here because I won't give them the satisfaction.
These people are beside themselves—

YOUNG DISCIPLE   What! Are you going to *discuss* it?

CASPAR (*Stubborn*)   Yes, I am. (*He reaches out and catches
a rock on the fly and shows it*) They have progressed to a
harder kind of tomatoes. (*He throws the rock down*)
They are beside themselves with astonishment because for
an instant Our Master showed them that something they
thought to be impossible was indeed possible. They are
affrighted out of their wits. Shall I therefore run away?

MELCHIOR   Our Master is dangerous because he is *not* a
magician, *not* a wonder-worker. The possibility of being
happy has them by the throat. One is irresistibly drawn
to do it. I have been irresistibly drawn to do it myself. So
he taught me. I blink. I draw a breath—
     (*He is showered with a handful of small stones*)

BALTHASAR   Poor folk, they are bitterly disappointed and
they have no one to reproach. Whom will they reproach?
I can sniff the murder in the air.
     (*Suddenly the* YOUNG DISCIPLE *darts into an alcove,
     grabs a man by the collar and drags him forth*)

YOUNG DISCIPLE   You! Don't worry, I won't hurt you. Your
teeth are chattering. What are you afraid of?

TOLERANT MAN   They say that he intends our advantage and
what he says will surely come to pass.

YOUNG DISCIPLE   But of course he intends your advantage!
What's wrong with that?

36

TOLERANT MAN (*Staring at him in terror and falling back*)
What's—wrong—with—*that?*
(*He turns in a panic and flees*)

CASPAR Come back, you! I want to *talk* to you— (*He
starts in pursuit but stumbles over the low rope and falls
flat. He picks himself up, shaking with rage. He is in a
towering anger*) Damn you! You have digged a pit! You
have digged a pit and you shall fall in it! (*The next moment he is crushed by melancholy; his shoulders droop.
The others stand near him in sympathy and are silent*)
My friends (*He reaches out and touches them*) —my
faith—you know—all of my faith comes down to simply
this: I can touch you—there is ground underfoot for a next
step. And so, having faith, I take a next step, I venture to
take a next step. How otherwise, friends, do we sing "Lead,
Kindly Light"? Lead, kindly light, amid the encircling
gloom, lead thou my steps, I do not ask to see the *distant*
scene; *one step* enough for me. (*He softly weeps*) I was
a strong man by standing on the ground underfoot and
there was always ground enough to support my two feet.
But now—

BALTHASAR (*Taking him in her arms*) Belovéd. No, you
shall not turn away, for we will *hound* you with our attention. Let me show you this rope better. Come look, it is a
rope. Do you remember? Of course! "The true way goes
over a rope, stretched at no great height but just above
the ground." Here it is, just as our friend Franz said. "It
is designed to make people stumble." Step over it. Like
this. (*She steps over it, and a stone bangs into the wall*)
So. (*He steps over*) What is hard about stepping over a
low rope?

37

(*Another stone hits and hurts her. She weeps, just for five seconds*)

CASPAR (*Like a child*)   Mother, are we to walk any further?

BALTHASAR   No. We are afraid. (*Tableau. Quartet. Now all four are trembling*) We are afraid: *how* are we afraid? This is as good a subject for our attention as any, we are not choosy. (*Another stone*) I wish they would stop throwing those stones, it is hard to be aware in the circumstances of life; it is impossible to be aware *not* in the circumstances of life. Let each one of us explain how he is afraid. First you.

CASPAR (*Very tired*)   I am afraid by being tired. So tired, my friends, trying where they don't want me. I am too tired to talk about it. Pass me by.
  (*He is hit by a stone, but is too tired to respond*)

MELCHIOR   I am afraid of this crowd because it is unintelligent. I don't know how to talk to faceless stones and I don't know what to expect from them. I don't know how to be easy with people except by keeping in touch with them. There, that's three times I've said the words "I don't know"—how should I know if I have no one to tell it to? (*Shouting*) Speak out! Ask me a question! *What* is it you want to know? (*A stone bangs against the wall*) It's your turn.

YOUNG DISCIPLE (*Sarcastically*)   Oh, sure, it's my turn. I'm afraid and they're afraid; and the pressing question is whether I'm more afraid of them than they are of me. Also, teacher, I know the answer. I'm more afraid of them than they are of me. They're stronger, and they have communicated to me their fear instead of my communicating to them my confidence. You see, we catch it! It's not with impunity that we go into all kinds of places—and what in hell are we doing *here*? Heads up!

(*He dodges out of the way and a big rock bangs against the wall. Another rock comes, and another*)

BOY (*Leaping from his hiding place*) For God's sake, what a pain in the ass you all are! You're afraid because they're throwing rocks at you and you stand there. Throw back! (*He picks up a rock and hurls it*) Lucky for us they have lousy aim because they have a bad conscience; they don't want to hurt us. But *I* don't have a guilty conscience.

(*He throws another rock*)

VOICE OFF STAGE Ouch! You little son of a bitch!

Curtain

The sound of a hunting horn. The curtain rises quickly on blackness. The hunting horn sounds, and sounds again.

Voice *of* OUR MASTER *in the Forest* (*Breathless*)
>All days are different days
>but there is one single night
>and she is called the Night,
>starlit or dark the Night,
>my black brain. I have wrapped
>myself around me like a coat
>or I would vanish shrieking in the night.
>I understand the werewolf, how he comes,
>opens his eyes and he can see at night,
>nor do things appear the same at night.
>(*The hunting horn again, in the distance. After a pause, enter the two Wise Men with lamps*)

CASPAR   Which way do you think he went?

MELCHIOR   It's no use. We can't catch up with him. He leaps ahead either as if he is hot on the trail or as if he is avoiding us. It comes to the same thing. Let's go back.

CASPAR   Did he say what he came out to hunt in the forest at night, when you can't see anything?

MELCHIOR   Yes. He is hunting the animal spirits where they withdraw after there has been a catastrophe. He is hunting in the moment after the catastrophe. He said he could not bring a light, for then they only withdraw the deeper. He is hunting what is still alive in the moment after the catastrophe. (*A distant horn*) There is his horn.

(*They pursue. Another corner of the stage. Blackness. The voice of* OUR MASTER *is heard making unintelligible whispered sounds, small squeals. Or perhaps he is carrying on a dialogue with another speaker, or several speakers. It is impossible to tell. Or perhaps it is just the whispering breeze in the foliage. Or he is talking to the animal spirits. Another part. Enter* MELCHIOR *holding the lantern high*)

MELCHIOR Hallooo! hallooo! (*He is lost*) Halloo! Where are you?

(*Finally there is an answer*)

CASPAR Here I am. Where are you? Hallooo!

(*After a moment he appears, across the scene*)

MELCHIOR (*Irritated*) I told you let's get out of here and go back. We're lost. That's all we need to end this lousy day, to get lost in the woods chasing a madman who is trying to avoid us.

CASPAR I thought I knew these woods letter-perfect, but everything looks different at night.

(*Exeunt, eclipsing the lamps*)

Curtain

ACT THREE

SCENE ONE

The barking of a dog like volleys of thunder. The curtain rises on dawn-blue, and at once a knife of sunlight. Enter the YOUNG DISCIPLE *gorgeously arrayed as Day.*

YOUNG DISCIPLE

>My family hound with ragged hair
>the Sun is barking thunderclaps,
>through all my house as home I come
>from lost in the underworld.
>
>"Up, sir!"—I pat his noble head
>of fire—"we'll go and hunt the Bear,
>I promised it if I returned,
>a *real* hunt if I came back!"
>(*A volley of barking and sunrise*)
>That dog is crazy with excitement,
>I am afraid for the furniture—
>"Quiet, sir! Down!"— I am confused,
>I am embarrassed by the dog
>flustered and flushing from pole to pole
>as home I come to my glad day.
>(*Silence. Pink*)
>Quiet, and it now stands still.
>And I recover my full height and bow,
>as toward me smiling and with outstretched arms
>slowly advances the lady my soul
>(*Music begins*)
>and red and pearly the dawn on my brow

has yielded to the unremitting glow
of everyday that starts in me,
and vibrates, and explodes.
(*Full day, and music for as long as it is beautiful*)
Explodes and persists.
                              I have
come down among the forest oaks
and where the deer have startled eyes
to the detail flower in the crannied wall
nor will I pluck the flower out of the cranny.
(*Scrim rises and it brightens as day comes there, revealing* OUR MASTER *seated in meditation*)
A hunter! under this dark ledge
with diagonal eyes of meditation
looks at me with a level look.
(*Hold the look for a rather long time. Then swiftly*)
Swiftly I creep behind his back
unstealthily—and stay—there—
but *you* are unalarmed and step
out on the familiar ground.
(*In contrast to the* YOUNG DISCIPLE, OUR MASTER *is dressed in plain stuff, poorly; the colors of it are stripes of bright and shadows—this Domino is man, across whose throat and shoulder a tag of daylight falls, across whose heart lies a night*)

OUR MASTER (*Always matter-of-fact*)   Yes. I step out on the familiar ground. You are my ground—for a step at a time. (*Lightly saluting the sun*) You are my star. And you, my world, you are lovely today! (*Noticing*) I cast a shadow. No, *I* don't cast it, but because I intervene, there is cast a night. So. (*He is speaking throughout not to himself but*

to his only world) I have reached that point in my meditation when I do or omit nothing at home that I would
not do away from home, and when I do or omit nothing
away from home that I would not do at home. I have no
home, it is home. So come, be amiable with your man
and let's make love.

> (*Noisily enter the Three Wise Ones—they do not
> confront* OUR MASTER *or address him—but they feel
> affronted by him, hurt, embarrassed, resentful. He
> neither avoids them nor confronts them, it is up to
> them; but he looks at them attentively enough—it is
> obvious that he is* not *avoiding them*)

CASPAR   He is *still* avoiding us! Why is he avoiding us?

MELCHIOR   Why don't you ask *him*? Why do you keep
looking at me? It's not written on *my* face.

CASPAR   Where are *you* looking? And you, madam!

BALTHASAR   What's the use? *You* know what he's saying to
himself?

CASPAR *and* MELCHIOR (*Fearfully*)   No. What?

BALTHASAR   He's saying, "They're afraid! They're afraid of
me, they're afraid of the people, they're afraid of the
night. They're afraid to be lost. How can I live with persons who are afraid?" And we *are* afraid. Who can deny
it? Yes! And then he goes on—

> (*Though they are crowded near* OUR MASTER, *they
> are paying him no attention at all. He keeps looking
> attentively from one speaker to another*)

CASPAR   Yes! Then he goes on and it's worse than anything.
He takes the blame on himself! I can't bear that. He says,

"It's my fault," he says. "If you're afraid of me, it means that I am not attentive enough to you; because there must be *some* way to speak to you that won't make you freeze up. What is it I do?" he asks. "Tell me. Do I talk too fast? Do I take too much for granted?"

MELCHIOR (*In suppressed fury*) Oh, yes! I know all that, I know what he means to say by *that*. I understand it only too well. He means to say that we are not *interesting* to him, we are not capable of conversing with him—and he has no one. But he swallows his disappointment. He doesn't want to hurt me, and so in order not to hurt me any further, he has begun to avoid me. *You* see how it is —it means— It means that he is no longer going to be himself—in power! "Temper the wind to the shorn lambs!" says he. Oooh (*Crushed*) Naturally he won't say this right out, it would hurt my feelings. But the fact that I understand it is enough. It is enough. He has come to a decision about all of us!

(*They are in consternation. Suddenly the light dims, to murky*)

MELCHIOR I seem to have gone blank.

CASPAR I blinked, and there was a blank.

ALL THREE Open your eyes.
(*It brightens*)

BALTHASAR Spiteful! Why do we want to make Our Master feel bad with our complaining? That isn't fair, is it? He has done well by us, but what does *he* get out of it? Think of that. What does *he* get out of it? All right, I accept that he isn't enlivened by us, that we aren't interesting to him. I am sorry for it—that I have nothing to give him—

because I love him. But then—why doesn't he look bored? Why doesn't he go away? Instead of looking bored, he looks sad. He looks sad and stays. Don't you think he looks sad?

CASPAR Of course, but I know the answer to that question. Where should he go? If he had some other world to go to, and not be here with us, he could allow himself to be bored, and he'd look bored, and he'd soon go away. But since we—alas!—are his only opportunity—because this is the only world there is, and we frustrate him—and we are not the worst!—what can he do but stand there, biting his lips—

(*And they stand and look at him; he is not biting his lips*)

OUR MASTER (*Passionately*) My only one! My world! (*Lightly*) Really, I must be in love if I persist so hard to be a happy man with you, with only you, my obsession. I cannot imagine another possibility than to keep making these idle passes at my only world.

BALTHASAR (*Awestruck*) He is taking us into account. Not only us, but also the fact that we are as we are.

MELCHIOR He is reveling in the fact that he is bored.

CASPAR He is gloating in the fact that we make him sad.

OUR MASTER (*A little childishly. In Quaker*) My darling, why does thee want to be so bitchy today? Thee don't keep thy promises. No, thee don't. Thee makes me expect a big day, and thee behaves like this. But I see thee has put on thy attractive daylight for me, the one I love, with the deep blue fur. Let's not quarrel, darling. But thee keeps turning thy face away. Say "thee" directly to me, the way I do to thee. I don't hold back, do I? Look, thee makes it hard for me to declare my honorable intentions. I like to have sex when I get up early in the morning fresh and new. That's when I feel like it. Thee knows that. (*Sorrowful and resigned*) And now thee goes through this business of putting thy hat on to go out! But thee can't get away with it, for, see, I'm following thee right out into the street and all the people are staring. (*Resolute, and making fun of his resolution*) Or suppose I decide to stay right here. Go ahead! I've had it. I've had enough, I say! Then thee has to stay too—for *here* thee are! (*Joyful*) And we end up with me weeping my heart out on the shoulder of my only world. I am in love not in vain. I always make out, whichever way it is! (*Angry*) Oh, this I despise! When you tell me in that tone, "Take it easy, guy!" Who in hell do you think you are? Damn you! How trivial can you get? You cock-teaser . . . O.K., I'll go down the street alone and leave you flat. I'll kick a stone along, the way I did when I was ten.

MELCHIOR (*Following to console him*)   Fellow! No! The god-damned bitch—

BALTHASAR (*Restraining him by the arm*)   Let be! Let be! Why don't you mind your own business?

CASPAR (*Angry*)   No, he's perfectly right. I've been through that myself.

BALTHASAR   I say, let be! It's in the nature of things.

CASPAR   Hush!

OUR MASTER (*As if chastened*)   I'm sorry. You didn't really promise me anything at all. You aren't really false, my world, my only one. You *are* puzzling, but you aren't mean. Who is to blame if I have unreasonable expectations? And thereby I miss out on what I indeed do have! Isn't it absurd? No, I'm content to be aware of just how it is with me here and now as I suffer, and now—see!—my dismay is turning slowly into glory as I walk away into my bawling solitude intent—and musical—and now I'll speak out music strong and sweet. We two are softly talking it over— (*There is music, an intimation of dance music, but without drums. Intimately*) You have come to me freely, no, my little one, my huge one? I'm not imposing anything on you, am I? Yes, whisper it—let us whisper. No one must hear except me and my only world, what we have to say to one another. So many things we have to say to one another.

(*The music dies away and his voice falls to an unintelligible whisper. And the* YOUNG DISCIPLE *rushes forward from the rear; his glorious array is torn*)

YOUNG DISCIPLE   I cannot deny it! I can't deny it any longer! The two of them are secretly whispering. They are whispering at my expense. Probably not *even* at my expense. They have left me *out*. I try to eavesdrop but it's in a foreign language, and there I crouch a bigger fool than ever. I could die. I am blind with envy. I've tried—I try to shut my eyes to it, but I can't blank out the scene. If I shut my eyes (*Directly confronting*) you have already begun to fuck in front of my face. If I force myself to keep my eyes open, it's not yet so bad as that. Not yet! Not yet! Don't! I'll open my eyes wide— (*Blackout. In a ringing voice*) Blind! Blind! It has smote me between the eyes, to see the possibility of natural satisfaction in the world.

(*Pause. When it brightens, the background has filled with all the persons of the play. The* YOUNG DISCIPLE, *among them, is without costume, as at the beginning. Dance music*)

OUR MASTER (*Gaily*) Shall *we* dance? May I have the next dance? Just try and say no! Oh, come, I know I have a hard-on; we aren't bashful. Thank you. Thank *you!*
(*He dances his Dance of Awareness of Himself and the Compresence of the Others*)

CASPAR (*Awestruck*) You are dancing down the street. You are holding close and joyfully to you the fact that people are astonished out of their wits.

MELCHIOR You are dancing away the fact that you have been wilting with boredom. You are holding close to you the fact that people are beside themselves with fear.

BALTHASAR Yes, you are sobbing for it on the shoulder of my only world and she is consoling you, as she can.

YOUNG DISCIPLE My friend! I can't help it—I am enchanted with you because you are not a waster of woe. You are simply dancing with delight the fact that I hate and envy you. (*Nauseated*) Let me go kill myself. The two of you are public and vulgar.
(*The music stops and the curtain falls*)

VOICE OF YOUNG DISCIPLE (*Loud, through the curtain*) What! You have withdrawn?! Is my criticism too harsh for you? Since when are we embarrassed to call a spade a spade? If *I* do not, *who* will do it? . . . (*Pleading but firm*) *Come* back! *Come* back! *Come* back, common day! (*Proud*) I ask it because I am adequate to it—if ever I

49

have braved the ignorant, and spoken, with pounding heart, the words that needed to be said.

(*The curtain rises. The music begins, a slow dance. And* OUR MASTER *dances his Dance of Fucking the Only World. After half a minute, while they dance*)

YOUNG DISCIPLE He is fucking with sober satisfaction the only situation that there is. (*After a pause*) Since I cannot deny it, let me confront it with wide eyes and say it to everybody: He is fucking with sober satisfaction the only situation that there is.

CASPAR Our Master is not a waster of his misery.

MELCHIOR He is not in love in vain, he makes out.

BALTHASAR

He is not a waster of his misery.
He is not in love in vain. He makes out.

YOUNG DISCIPLE

This time, I think, he has made her pregnant.
Too late—even if I wanted to do that—
it is too late to intervene and prevent it.
In spite of my dismay, my penis is rising, too.

(*Passionately*) My darling one! My world, whom must I love, if I so hard persist and pursue to become a happy man with you, just you, with only you, my obsession. For I cannot imagine another possibility than to keep making such idle passes at my only world. Whisper it to me? What word must *I* whisper? Lovely! And what colors shall I wear? Where must I stand and wait to catch you in the mood?

(*All together*)

VOICE

Beloved! Speak to me.

CHORUS (*Softly*)

Let us practice softly
the pronouns You and We.

VOICE

Only these are true.

CHORUS

All questions and commands
have as meaning You,
and proud and glad are We.

VOICE

So let us utter only
the pronouns You and We.

CHORUS

Only these are true.

VOICE

My questions and commands

CHORUS

have as meaning You.
Proud and glad are We!

VOICE

Beloved! Speak to me!

CHORUS (*Strong*)

The pronouns You and We—
Only these are true!
(*Piano, subito. Hushed*)
Are you pregnant, my only world?
Whisper it in my ear.

VOICE

Are you pregnant, my only world?
Whisper it in my ear.

CHORUS (*Strong and solemn*)
Oh, awesome is the hour
—that everyone forgets—
when we let go ourself
that you may come to be.
But proud and glad are we
to be lost, to be lost.

Quick curtain

Prelude: The following song is for baritone voice with the music of Ned Rorem.

VOICE (*Singing*)
>I thought I woke: the Midnight Sun
>>flooded the street among the trees,
>>the people floated at their ease
>to right and left, I moved alone.

>A savage drone, the thrilling air
>>of bagpipes poured around the bend,
>>the valley echoed end to end,
>I hastened to behold him there.

>The meaning of dreams in this magic day
>>was clear as they befell, without
>>the need or use to think it out;
>and where the shadows fell they lay.
>(*Here the song ends. The* VOICE *continues, declaiming*)

VOICE

>Where the shadows fell they lay—

>shapes of gold leaf that dully burn,
>>such shapes the travelers display
>as souvenirs when they return:
>>"These are the shadows as they lay,

>"We gathered them, this jumping mishap
>>and this grotesque profile,

53

this crooked hand is a common shape
stretching a startling mile."

*The curtain rises, looking into the room of a country
tavern with a window, a door and a few steps downward into
the street. The* YOUNG DISCIPLE *is in bed, in pyjama bottoms.*

The BOY, *his valet, is busy laying out his clothes.*

YOUNG DISCIPLE (*Sitting up*) My head—ooh, my head.
What a night! Is there any coffee? Where in *hell* was I
yesterday? Ugh! (*He is nauseated*) I've got to give up
these hours. I can't take it any more. I wish to God I
were home. (*The* BOY *brings a cigarette, lights it*) Every
morning I wake up with a more vivid picture—home,
home! Mama! Even papa! Suddenly we'll just pack up
and leave, no? What in *hell* am I doing in this provincial
place? Come to think of it, what *am* I doing here? Boy!

BOY   Sir?

YOUNG DISCIPLE (*Definitely*) Look. Somebody has spread a
rumor that I came here following some magician or
wonder-worker, I don't know what, a native fakir. I've
never seen this man, I'm not curious about such things.
Did *you* have anything to do with spreading this rumor?

BOY   I, sir? No, I spread no such rumor.

YOUNG DISCIPLE   I believe you. Yet, it's curious, and I don't
like it.

BOY   Why, what is it to you what they say? Are you
ashamed to be associated with such things?

YOUNG DISCIPLE (*Urbane*) Ashamed? I think you misunder-
stand me. I don't for a moment doubt that such things

exist—some persons *have* extraordinary powers—then why not this village magician? I'm not skeptical by character . . . But I'm certain, certain as that I sit here, that such extraordinary powers are of no use to humane society. They talk to the spirits but they never get any useful information . . . Are you making the coffee?

BOY Coming up, sir.

YOUNG DISCIPLE No. The question is why they connect him with *me*. It seems there is some kind of social upheaval going on here—*you* would know, kids know everything— a crisis, rival factions. The group opposed to magus—and it seems to be the majority—is wildly suspicious of every stranger. And besides I have money and breeding and education. Therefore—do you follow me?

BOY Yes, sir, you're right, sir.

YOUNG DISCIPLE I wonder what they suspect. Such projections are damnably interesting. These people simply *cannot* accept that a man is on his travels. But perhaps they are right—the people is always right!—for *why* is he?

BOY Why is who?

YOUNG DISCIPLE Why *is* a man on his travels?

BOY Is the people always right? I'm surprised to hear you say so.

YOUNG DISCIPLE Always, always, always. I've inquired among the crowd, you know, the way I do—in the taverns till I get too lit myself; most of my headaches come from social science. The salient fact—it strikes you in the face— is that these people are *bitterly* disappointed. It's as if —as if somebody had promised them something, a solution, a way out—and then he let them down. They're at their wits' end, the way you get a woman heated up and then don't come across. (*Avuncular*) You mustn't do that, boy. Understand? The basic virtue of a gentleman is to come across. No excuses.

BOY   I agree, sir.

YOUNG DISCIPLE   Otherwise, don't mess around . . . Next thing they attribute their disappointment to this magician, and that's why all the furor against *him*. Well, if so, they are unjust, for so far as I have been able to discover—and I've gone into this too—the magus doesn't concern himself with politics. Yet *why* doesn't he? Maybe that's just the point! Maybe the crowd is in the right! I'm full of questions today. Why is a man on his travels? And why doesn't the magus concern himself with politics?

BOY (*Serving*)   Your coffee, sir.

YOUNG DISCIPLE   Thank you. Why are you surprised that I say the crowd is in the right? In my experience it is always right in the essentials, in the deep motives—for to perceive these requires only feeling, and this the crowd has, it has soul. But of course in everything else, in the detail, in the discriminating means, in the right measure, in the efficient, in the tolerant, et cetera, et cetera, the crowd is invariably in the wrong; for to hit this, you've got to *know*; and how should *they* know? Do you follow me?

BOY   Yes, sir.

YOUNG DISCIPLE   You're a bright boy.

BOY   Thank you, sir.
        (*Pause, while the* YOUNG DISCIPLE *sips his coffee*)

YOUNG DISCIPLE   Anyway, about this magus—if anybody asks
you—I don't know him, I never met him, no comment,
et cetera, et cetera. Do you understand?

BOY   Perfectly, sir.
    (*There is a noise off stage, and a forerunner of the*
    CROWD *comes pounding at the door*)

YOUNG DISCIPLE   What the hell? (*A rock flies through the*
window) There you are. Good morning! Nice morning,
isn't it? Just as I expected. There's your crowd for you.
Stones, too. (*He looks out the window*) What a hullabaloo! I despise this kind of ruckus. What in hell am I
supposed to say to them. (*Two or three more have ar-*
rived outside. Loud pounding. The BOY *looks at him help-*
lessly) Open the door. Get it over with. You know, it
makes no difference what they accuse me of, I always feel
guilty beforehand anyway.
    (*The* BOY *opens the door*)

PART OF CROWD   Where is the foreigner?
    (*Another rock*)

YOUNG DISCIPLE   (*Coming briskly forward*) What do you
want? Can't you knock civilly? Stop throwing those rocks
or I'll go out and boot you in your two hundred asses.
(*He looks out the window*) Oh, isn't that too bad! Look,
boy, they have the poor wretch there in chains. (*A knot
of the* CROWD *pressing from the wings with the chained
man, his back to the audience*) *There* you can see it!
Spread out like a picture. Hooting and mocking and sadistic: frightened out of their wits at themselves, at
themselves, and dreaming up God knows what dreams.
I hate mankind. But they are bitterly disappointed, bit-

terly! (*At the door, looking out toward the audience, addressing the* CROWD) Aren't you ashamed of yourselves? Howling to work up a little excitement between the cradle and the grave? How repulsive you are in your spite! I am not afraid of you.

MAN OF CROWD   Foreigner! Do you know this man?

YOUNG DISCIPLE   No.

CROWD   He's lying. He's lying. I saw them whispering together.

OTHER PART OF CROWD   This one crossed the water wi' the other one on his back.

ANOTHER PART   What the hell are you doing here in our town? Why don't you go back where you came from?

ANOTHER PART   Speak up! You'll get what's coming to you, too.

ANOTHER PART   Your turn's next!

YOUNG DISCIPLE   Bravo! bravo! You impress me with your wisdom and daring. No, I don't know this man, I've never talked to him, but I'd sooner know him and be his friend than a thousand heroes like you torturing one harmless fool. *Lay your hands off!* (*Sotto voce aside*) Here I go again! What business *is* it o' mine? *Step back! Back,* I say—

> (*He comes at them threateningly down the steps and for a moment they fall back. In an instant, with arms uprearing big clubs and rocks, they have crushed to death* OUR MASTER's *earthly head and frame*)

BOY *and* YOUNG DISCIPLE (*In astonished horror*) Ohhh! (*An indrawn gasp*) I can't believe my eyes.
>(*The scene dims. There is a pause. The* YOUNG DISCIPLE *is suddenly in the* CROWD *in the street. He cries out*)

YOUNG DISCIPLE You have killed a saint!
>(*A pause*)

YOUNG DISCIPLE *and* CROWD We have killed a saint!

YOUNG DISCIPLE The Glory is eclipsed out of our world!

YOUNG DISCIPLE *and* CROWD Eclipsed out of our world.

YOUNG DISCIPLE We are confronting one another in demi-darkness.
>(*He stands away from them*)

THREE OF THE CROWD He went across the water!

ANOTHER THREE She was dead.

YOUNG DISCIPLE (*As if under a spell*) Yes, he went across the water and she was dead.
>(*At this moment the* BOY *begins to bawl in the doorway. A spot shines on the* YOUNG DISCIPLE)

YOUNG DISCIPLE (*To the* BOY) Boy! Was it I who said that idiotic sentence? But I am *aware* of what I am doing! I cannot help it. The soul of the people is irresistible; I shall not foolishly try to resist it. Even so I shall with sober satisfaction say in words exactly how it was and how it is. I shall continue to do that. (*The* BOY *is sobbing*) I am aware how I denied him. (*The* BOY *is sobbing*) I have been astonished *not* out of my wits. I am almost at home here with these superstitious people. I do not love them yet, but that will come in time. And found our church.

(*But the* BOY *is sobbing, inconsolable, nor is there any consolation. He begins to pound on the wall. His grief is turning into a tantrum. He rolls on the ground, kicking with his feet and pounding with his fists and roaring. The curtain comes quickly down, across him. In his tantrum he tears at it and pulls it half from its rings. He subsides*)

Blackout

Again, to Ludwig van Beethoven

Comment on *The Young Disciple*

This little martyr-play is grounded in the method of textual criticism of Martin Buber, especially his *Moses*. When a startling event has occurred, the community strives to interpret it, to blot it out, to mythologize it, so that life can go on as ordinary; and what survives to us as a record is the history not of the event, but of the panic response of the community to the event. This is not different in principle, it seems to me, from Bergson's account of evolution as the record of the reactions of matter to the stress of the *élan vital*.

To imitate this reactive process in its purity, I have made the "miraculous event" consist precisely in what is most ordinary, namely, what is the case.

I came to this play through a psychological analysis of the Gospel of Mark. In this book, what powerfully strikes a psychologist is the profusion of expressions of being beside oneself with fear and confusion. "They were affrighted," "they were frightened out of their wits," "they were stunned," "they were astonished," "they were had by trembling and ecstasy." Every story of the nonnatural will of course have such expressions—as dogs, in the *Proceedings* of the Society for Psychical Research, tend to have raised ruffs and tremble —but Mark is so profuse in them that the reader feels he is pretty close to the hidden event itself, the thing that "makes no sense."

I would interpret the "secrecy" in Mark in the same direction. Unable to cope with "I don't know," men screw up their eyes and say, "I won't tell."

I have tried in this play to lay emphasis on the pre-verbal elements of theatre: outcries and gasping, bawling and giggling, trembling, breathing hard, throwing tantrums and throwing punches. Unfortunately, the actors we have are quite unable, both by character and training, to open their throats to such sounds or loosen their limbs to such motions. This is also why they cannot simply read poetic lines. It would be worthwhile—if only to the renovation of theatre as an art—to make a number of plays of just these pre-verbal elements in abstraction, as the painters have returned to the elements of pure color and composition.

Lastly, here as elsewhere, I have tried to study a little further the scenic situation itself, this time the lights and the curtain. And I am disturbed, looking back at the ending that I wrote, at how desperate the artist's plight has now come to seem to me.

New York City
October 1954

Faustina

Characters

FAUSTINA

CORNELIA

MARCUS AURELIUS

FRONTO

GALBA

MESSENGER

FIRST SOLDIER

SECOND SOLDIER

ISIS

BOY

ROMAN CHORUS

SPOKESMAN

ACT ONE

An empty platform. Right, toward the rear, a steep flight of seven steps with an exit at the top. Front, toward the left, an exit forward down. In the back a little left of center, a window. Front right, a screen or wings. This scene is the body of the empress: the seven vertebrae of the neck leading to the head, the eyes looking out, the vagina toward us, the secrecy of the breast.

There is a roaring of beasts from the arena. ANNIA FAUS-TINA, *Empress of Rome, aged thirty-six, is at the window.* CORNELIA, *an elderly matron, is nearby.*

FAUSTINA I will not look again! (*Gasping, she hurls herself away from the window*) What is he doing?

CORNELIA (*At the window*) Now he is closing with the spotted bear, the crazy one they sent from Scythia.

FAUSTINA How will he hew his way into that thing—all hairs?

CORNELIA See for yourself.

FAUSTINA No, I cannot. See for me.
(*Shouts from outside*)

CORNELIA He has fallen on his back. Ow, my weak eyes! (*She shies away*) His sword is like a mirror, and the sun—

FAUSTINA Yes, I saw the stripe on your face—

CORNELIA I don't think he's much hurt. But there's blood there.

FAUSTINA *What* blood?

CORNELIA *Mixed* blood. (*More shouts outside*) I see, he threw himself *underneath* the animal—

FAUSTINA A softer place, where the hair is thin—
(*Shouts, fanfare*)

CORNELIA The thing has fallen over on its side.
(*Pause*)

FAUSTINA Is this the moment when he turns the sword?

CORNELIA This is the moment when he usually turns the sword. Ugh. He is turning it—as if in vengeance. Revenge for what? There is a lot of blood. I will not look.
(*She draws away. After a moment,* FAUSTINA *rushes to the window and cries out*)

FAUSTINA

Feast, my lewd eyes!
give way to it, my soul!
Hot hungering,
you reaching brats,

Take what is on the table,
take everything, only shut up'
I will to be at peace.
And now I am at peace.

Am I at peace? O come away
into my raging insides.
(*She flees front and down, exit. There is laughter behind the screen*)

CORNELIA (*Angrily*)

Young idiots, jeer!—and afterward? What then?
When you are old and this dream has passed away,

this kind of dream, you will not easily
find another error to believe.

And yet I understand them—here all of us are wise—
they stumble headlong into their next step
as she does into hers, and I in mine.
(*The door opens at the top of the steps*)
But the Emperor, Marcus Aurelius—
(MARCUS *and* FRONTO *appear in the high door.* MAR-
CUS AURELIUS, *Emperor of Rome, in his late forties,
speaks gravely, gravely sad, gravely mirthful. The
words are pedantic, but not the manner.* FRONTO *is
considerably older.* FRONTO *precedes him downstairs.*
MARCUS *begins to speak at the top and descends slowly, while* FRONTO *waits*)

MARCUS Fronto! What must I tell myself, when I talk to
myself seriously? Say, "Marcus! Remember how long you
have already put off these things; how often, when a certain day and a certain hour was appointed by the gods,
you have neglected it. It is high time to understand the
true nature of the world you are a part of! There is only
a certain limit of time given you; if you do not make use
of this to calm the diseases of your soul, it will pass away,
and you with it, and never return again."

FRONTO Must you tell this to yourself? Might you not tell
it to me, or to any man? It's not a very personal item of
news.

MARCUS No, to myself, to myself. What right have I to advise or reprimand somebody else? I must tell myself about
the small things, Fronto, the everyday things, that press
evenly and continuously. I am not going to tell myself

67

about the world and the stars and the first principles—
but about how I carry my shoulders, and the tone of voice
I speak in, and what images I let flash into my mind, and
what have I learned day by day from my friends.

FRONTO   I am your friend, Marcus. What have you learned
from me?

MARCUS   What have I learned from Fronto? It was Fronto
who pointed out to me that kings and senators, those who
are commonly called nobly born, that such people are
incapable of natural affection.

FRONTO   Did you have to be told this? You could have
noticed it yourself.

MARCUS   I notice very little myself, I am not quick. But I
learn from other people.

FRONTO   What did you learn from—from your father?

MARCUS   From my father? What small thing did I learn
from him who brought me up? Yes! Look here. (*He goes
to the window*) I remember. At the circuses and games,
my father taught me to be impartial, to look on without
fanaticism, not to grow hot for this horse or that horse,
for this gladiator or against—*this* gladiator.
(*Exeunt left.* FAUSTINA *enters from front, half clad,
and as if raving*)

FAUSTINA

This space is my body; why is the world
—how dares it—trooping in here carelessly?
It is no shame that I have come from down
in that pit nearer where the lions roar.
My thoughts are yonder at the top of seven

steps. But draw, O draw the curtain over
and shut the world out.
(CORNELIA *draws the curtain*)
Where are my children? How am I justified?

CORNELIA

Madam, the boy is taken to the camp to be a man.

FAUSTINA

Are you still here? Was it the Emperor
who passed discoursing by? I heard his gentle voice
and I have reappeared from my lair
to be reminded of something I forgot.

CORNELIA

The Emperor and Fronto walked that way.

FAUSTINA

Aiiiiiiiiiii—
hold me—my head is splitting in two halves.
(CORNELIA *supports her. More calmly*)
Mother, if I believed,
if I believed in such vindictive witches,
I would believe that Aphrodite or
a she-devil with a Babylonian name
has taken me to be a drum to beat on
in order that people might not forget the noise
of crazy longing in this ordered universe.
(*Listening to herself*)
There is a big, repeated belly-boom—
and fluttering tapping—don't you hear anything?
What does it want to say?
But why should I lie and make up fables?
It's my own pulse pounding in my own head.

Am I the wife of Marcus Aurelius
the philosopher, and am I the Empress of Rome?
Why do I feel heavy in the air,
in the empty corridors where he is not,
the body of the gladiator Galba,
and it is important to me that he kills a bear?
Answer me that.

CORNELIA

Child, may I speak?

FAUSTINA

Speak.

CORNELIA

Often fears vanish when we take them close,
their whole existence is in our avoiding.

FAUSTINA

I do not understand. Be more explicit.

CORNELIA

His body is your fear. Take it close.

FAUSTINA (*Coldly*)

I understand. Be more explicit still.

CORNELIA

You are angry, madam. I am not afraid.

FAUSTINA

You fool! What are you imagining,
and what are you not imagining?
I am Faustina, is this hard for me,
to rearrange the bodies of the Romans?
From what bed do you think I've stepped half dressed?
He comes to me in the hot afternoons
directly—

when the excitement is alive in him,
when the excitement is alive in both of us.
This brown stain is the blood of the animal.
(*She bares her side*)
I know what he can do, such as it is.
He has a penis like another man,
no bigger and less learned than my husband's—
Why do you pale?

CORNELIA

                I am afraid of you.
Although I have lived many years on the earth—

FAUSTINA

On what earth? Do you think I'd have recourse
to words and make up fables about gods
if I had not experimented the simple thing?

CORNELIA (*Pause*)

What do you complain of? I am lost.
You are in love, and you give way to it,
and what you want you have. Is something more?
Another woman would be happy so!

FAUSTINA   Another woman is not the Empress of Rome.

See how it streaks!
Like winking fire in the dry grass!
Sporadically, and under the footsteps
about the ankles, look—!

CORNELIA

              What are you seeing?

FAUSTINA

Laughter! Unheard, because they do not dare,
crinkling silently behind their ears.

71

All right! We are ridiculous! Laugh loud,
say a word about Marcus Aurelius!
Let in the world!
(*She tears down the curtain*)
          My uncle built these Baths
for general pleasure, not for privacy—
are we not parts of one another?
(*There are loud laughs in the wing*)
The laughter is *behind* my back!
Where? Where is it? Let *me* see the teeth!

CORNELIA

    Is the Empress afraid of ridicule?
These are two slaves, thwarted in everything.
What shall they do but laugh?

FAUSTINA (*Reverie*)

               Are there such things?
Is this, perhaps, why he *turns* the sword?
(*She sinks to the ground, as if in a swoon. But when*
CORNELIA *comes to aid her, she leans on her elbow*
and begins factually—but with mounting hysteria)
Madam, let me anatomize my state,
clearer to you than it has been to me.
My head is yonder and my bowels down there,
and when I turn to look out on the world
there is a burst of laughter behind my back.
Here in the middle they have taken away
my children and left me an empty space.
There is a menace in the corridors
and blood on my left flank, and all the world
is trooping carelessly through the hall,
while Aphrodite pounds on the drums!

My uncle built these Baths for general pleasure—
Begin! Your mother is a house, a city,
and she has seven hills! They are old.
Old! Old! Your mother is a-moldering.
Now I am walking on the flowery ways
to Appia and Brindisi and the south—

CORNELIA

Your Majesty—

FAUSTINA (*Rising, coldly*)

It is impossible
to be so and be the Empress of Rome.
First I must learn somewhat to be myself.
Why should I lie? I will to be avenged.

CORNELIA

Avenged on whom? For what? What has he done
otherwise than you yourself commanded?

FAUSTINA

Because I am not mistress of myself
avenged on him, avenged on myself.

CORNELIA

Will vengeance make you mistress of yourself?

FAUSTINA

No, but the insult of living is
too gross to bear without retaliation.

VOICE OF GALBA (*From in front*)

Annia!

FAUSTINA

Why, I am coming.
We shall yet see which of us turns the sword.

73

(*Exit front. Re-enter* MARCUS *and* FRONTO *from the left. Two following* SOLDIERS *post themselves against the wall. While* MARCUS *speaks, a* MESSENGER *tries to gain his attention*)

MARCUS   From Sixtus? What did I learn from Sixtus? From Sixtus, mildness and the pattern of a family governed with paternal affection; and the purpose to live according to nature—those things surely—

MESSENGER   Sir—

MARCUS (*Brushing him away*)   Do you know what I really learned from Sixtus, Fronto? I learned not to be offended with idiots! And especially this, not to set on them with the theorems and tenets of philosophers to lay them low! His conversation was a model of how to accommodate to all men and to all companies. (*The* MESSENGER *tries to draw him aside*) Please, sir, speak publicly. There is nothing that concerns me privately. The Empress—?

MESSENGER (*Embarrassed*)   The Empress Faustina—and— I mean—
        (FRONTO *turns to leave*)

MARCUS   Fronto!

FRONTO   There is nothing that concerns you privately. Also there are some things that do not concern me to hear.

MARCUS (*Firmly*)   I beg your pardon, you will stay. Why are *you* to be spared the pains that come of my living as a social being? Speak up, man, without embarrassment. Inform me—I know what you have to inform me: "The Empress Faustina is again copulating with the gladiator Galba. He is lying on her; or she is lying on him; or they

are lying side by side—however it happens to be." There!
Is that hard to speak out? They are words like any others.
Soldier! Your name is Publius; we fought together in the
north. Are you afraid to cause pain to your friends? Only
to enemies? Rest assured, you do not cause me pain.

(*Exit* MESSENGER. FRONTO *again tries to leave*)

MARCUS Fronto! From Alexander the Platonic, do you
know what I learned? He taught me that I must not often
say, or write, in a letter: "I am not at leisure; I am too
busy"—putting off what we owe our friends and acquaint-
ances, every one in his kind, pretending that there is
something more urgent. Fronto, have you the leisure for
me now?

FRONTO I have the leisure.

MARCUS It is not true, what I said to the boy. What advantage is it to lie to myself? What he informed me, what
I informed myself, has caused me pain. I am surprised at
this. Also I do not like how I painted the scene of it, so
vividly, to myself—

FRONTO Aurelius! Look away; do not watch now!

(*He draws back into the shadow. Enter* GALBA *from
front, bewildered*)

GALBA What the devil! What's this place? She is making
a fool of me? She told me to come this way! (*He speaks
to* CORNELIA) Old woman, did the Empress Faustina pass
by here? (CORNELIA *shakes her head*) She said she would
lie here, I'd find her here, waiting. It was a whim of hers.
Surely she didn't expect us to screw on the floor, in a
public gallery, with the whole world trooping in and out.

CORNELIA You speak intimately of that lady.

75

GALBA I am the gladiator Galba. There is no secret of it . . . She said her knees would loom apart like the Aventine and the Janiculum; and I could clamber there like a small boy, because she was a giantess. And that her head would be above the clouds.

  (*He laughs*)

CORNELIA You have a pleasant speech, boy, and a strong body. But you ought not to laugh; it's ugly.

GALBA Why shouldn't I laugh, old lady? Isn't this what they laugh about?

  (*He laughs boisterously*)

CORNELIA Do you mean to laugh, or are you just following the others like an ape?

GALBA (*Soberly*) You're right. I don't mean it. There is something they don't understand. But why should I think any different from the rest?

MARCUS (*From the shadow*) What must I tell myself? Say, "Marcus, remember always to make a precise description and a careful drawing of every object that presents itself to your mind, in order wholly and thoroughly to contemplate it, in its proper nature, bare and naked. Divide it up into its proper parts and quarters and then—to yourself in your mind—call it and each of the parts it consists of by their proper and true names. For there is nothing so effective in begetting a true magnanimity as to be able *truly* and *methodically* to consider all things that happen in this life."

  (*As he speaks,* GALBA *is awestruck, frozen*)

GALBA It is the Emperor, I have heard of this—how he talks.

76

(*He begins to tremble.* MARCUS *approaches him and looks at him*)

MARCUS You say you are the gladiator Galba. I have not seen you before.

GALBA I am he.
(*Trembling violently, he falls to his knees*)

MARCUS Stand up. What are you afraid of? Do you tremble like that in the face of the jaws of the beasts? Maybe you do. I have sometimes shaken myself into a daring action. Stand up.

GALBA I have not wronged the animal beforehand. I do not feel guilty in the arena, so I am not afraid.

MARCUS Wronged? Guilty? What are these strange words? Oh, you must not act reluctantly! I mean, if there is something you partly do not want to do, you must not do it at all till you make up your mind; otherwise you do damage to yourself . . . You have not wronged *me*, though I have caused myself pain on your account; but that's not your doing. Stand up.

GALBA (*Simply*) I would stand up if my knees weren't too weak to hold me up.

MARCUS (*To* FRONTO) Support him. How can I talk equally to him if he is on his knees and I am standing; and I will not fall to *my* knees.

FRONTO Come, stand before the Emperor of Rome. (GALBA *bursts into tears.* FRONTO *says sharply to* MARCUS) Another man would be satisfied to see his rival remorseful and abased and not look for a more methodical revenge.

MARCUS I do not feel any revenge.

FRONTO You feel very little. I know you better than you know yourself.

(MARCUS *examines the gladiator*)

MARCUS You fuck my wife. Why do you? Because she is the Empress?

GALBA (*Indignant*) No, that's a lie! I mean—I did—what you say—but not for that reason.

MARCUS Then why?

GALBA Why? You know why. I—I don't know how to say it. A lay.

MARCUS A woman? Just any woman?

GALBA No, but many women. She—she's not the first, nor the second, nor—I'm not boasting, it's just how it is. Besides, she's my type. I like her.

MARCUS What is your type?

GALBA I can tell you that! I like cunt that is pretty, hot and intelligent. Ones who have a good time. Also, if they're a little older than me, and they teach me something. Annia is smart, sometimes she tries to make a fool of me. I'm not smart, but I'm not a fool. I know what the score is.

MARCUS Do you have a good time with such women, if they're your type?

GALBA Yes, I do, if she's my type. Sometimes I have a wonderful party.

MARCUS Oh? A wonderful party! I don't know these words. And—is that how you live?

GALBA What do you mean? I don't dig.

MARCUS I mean, whenever such women are available, the ones you like, you fuck them, and sometimes you have a wonderful party? Is that the way of it?

GALBA Yes, that's how it is. That's the way I live . . . Thanks.

MARCUS Thanks? Why do you thank me?

GALBA You make it so simple and clear. One part after another.

MARCUS . . . Fronto, *are* there such things?

GALBA Your Majesty, isn't that the way *you* live? . . . Oh, but I see that for you everything is available. I guess you get sick of it.

MARCUS Do you get sick of it?

GALBA (*Positively*) No. I never have too much.

MARCUS So. You seem to know something of what you want. Tell me, did you ever hear of the Greek Socrates?

GALBA No, who's he?

MARCUS He died long ago. He was killed. He used to say—

GALBA Who killed him?

MARCUS That's a long story. But he used to say, "Know thyself." That's the most important thing there is, to know yourself. And from what you say, you seem to know yourself.

GALBA Oh, no! Not me! That's hard; that's not easy. You'd be surprised. You do the god-damnedest things! But did he say it was the *most* important thing. I don't think so. Hmm. The most important thing. It's a thought—
(*Pause*)

MARCUS You please me, gladiator. I love you. (*Abruptly*) They say you turn the sword in the wound.

GALBA What? (*Indignant*) There that goes again! I don't! I don't! Do you hear me? I don't!

FRONTO What do you mean, you don't?

GALBA I don't turn any sword. Are you talking about the gladiator Galba? Why should I turn the sword—the beast is dying, or dead—I don't know what! Who are you talking about? It's a lie! Lie!

FRONTO The man is lying. I have seen it.

GALBA I am not lying. They're envious. (*He jeers and laughs*) Naturally they say anything they can. What can they say? But the crowd roars when Galba steps on the sand. Then the black cat springs—
    (*He feints*)

CORNELIA (*Quietly*) He turns the sword.

GALBA Damnation! You old bitch! Are you jealous too? What are *you* jealous about?

SOLDIERS Your Majesty, he's lying. It's plain as day.

GALBA (*Hopelessly, as if crazed*) What is this? I suppose you saw it too?

MARCUS (*To the others*) Please. The man is not lying. One does not lie in front of twenty thousand eyes, at high noon, under the sunlight.

GALBA Yes, they all can see.

MARCUS Nevertheless, Galba, you turn the sword.

GALBA You too? Emperor? (*Crafty*) Ah, I see. You think I'm crazy.

MARCUS (*Simply*)   Yes, I do. You do it and you don't know you do it.

GALBA (*Smiling broadly*)   Excuse me—but what you say— (*He laughs involuntarily*) I'm ashamed, I don't mean to laugh at you, but— (*He chokes*) and these people.
(*He roars with laughter*)

MARCUS   It's all right, boy, I'm not afraid to be ridiculous . . . Gladiator, can you play-act? The way you did before, feinting with the black cat?

GALBA   Yes, I can play-act.

MARCUS (*Almost enthusiastic*)   Good! Let us play out the Death in the Arena! Can you dance? Let's dance it, you and I. I am the beast. What beast shall I be? I am the Black Tiger. (*Growls, and laughs gravely*) And you must play the gladiator Galba. That's an easy part, you know it well. But Fronto, you must be the critic. You must judge if we imitate it right!

FRONTO   I am the critic.

MARCUS   Give him a pointless sword. (*A soldier breaks off a point and gives the stump of the sword*) Are you ready, Gladiator?
(MARCUS *makes a bestial sound and begins to dance the Tiger*)

GALBA   What must I do? Ah. So.
(*He begins to dance the Gladiator*)
So. I see the jaws
of Happy Arabia
slavering, and I am quivering.
But an Italian sword
can set my people free!

SECOND SOLDIER
> Yes! An Italian sword
> will set my people free!

FIRST SOLDIER (*Sotto voce*)
> By Jesus! Hold your tongue.

MARCUS (*Menacing the* SOLDIERS)
> I have more teeth than these,
> rank upon rank in darkness.
> (*He pounces,* GALBA *avoids him*)

GALBA
> Beast! Open wide
> from the ground to the sky.
> Here is the gate of Hell.
> Tigers I kill head-on,
> my iron down the throat.

FIRST SOLDIER
> Oh, it is blinding hot.

SECOND SOLDIER
> The noise is making me sick.

GALBA (*Preparing the* coup de grâce)
> Now. I dedicate
> this to the Queen of Love.
> (*He thrusts*)

SECOND SOLDIER   Hurrah!

FRONTO   Stop! It is a false imitation of the reality. Gladiator, hold your posture. Do not move. This is not the way you stand in the arena at the coup de grâce. I have watched it closely.

GALBA   Why, what's wrong? It is exactly so.

FRONTO   Not so. Look at his open mouth. In the arena the teeth are tight with the underlip drawn in as if he would bite it through. Look, here are the toothmarks.
(*He draws in a hiss*)

GALBA   (*Innocently imitating*)   Like this?
(*He hisses*)

FRONTO   Raise the shoulders narrowly together and the head sinks in the pit. Reach forward.

GALBA   Like this?

FRONTO   Yes, do it! Do it! Right! Now dare to act it out. Right elbow close.
(*Pause.* GALBA *is paralyzed in the posture. Then, hissing violently inward, he thrusts.* MARCUS *falls to his knees with a groan*)

FRONTO   Watch now!
(GALBA *moves entranced, as if his arm and sword were no part of himself.* MARCUS *rises—*GALBA *chokes in rage and horror*)

SOLDIERS   (*Awestruck, revolted, softly*).   He is turning the sword.
(CORNELIA *hides her face in her robe. The sword drops to the ground.* GALBA *falls to his knees. He sobs low and, after a while, bitterly.* MARCUS *stands inquisitorially over him. The* SECOND SOLDIER *sobs, and his sword falls to the ground*)

MARCUS   Vindictive slave! On what do you revenge yourself?

83

GALBA   On everything, on everything.

MARCUS   (*Relenting*)   Poor hurt child, what is the matter?

GALBA   I hate *myself*.

MARCUS   Are you taking revenge on the Emperor of Rome? (GALBA *sobs*) Is it for this reason that you abuse my wife Faustina? Because she is the Empress and my wife? (*Silence. Then, sadly*) But you said that it was not for this reason. You do not know yourself. Go and consider it. Go. Go.

GALBA   (*In a changed voice, as if wondering*)   Why did she tell me she'd wait for me here? She is nowhere! Not here!

FRONTO   Arrest that man!
         (SOLDIERS *drag* GALBA *to his feet*)

MARCUS   Set that man free!

FRONTO   Marcus, be advised. Arrest him—and send him away—before you take a more signal revenge.

MARCUS   Lead him out. Let him go free in Rome. Tomorrow he will again fight in the arena, if he so pleases.
         (SOLDIERS *lead* GALBA *out*)

FIRST SOLDIER   So, are you content?

SECOND SOLDIER   No! I am *not* content.

FRONTO   Marcus Aurelius! Consider it yourself. The man is not free, nor can you set him free any more. You are not free yourself; there is no one free in Rome. Why is the man taking vengeance on inoffensive beasts? "For everything! For everything!" He has much to take vengeance on, from the cradle to the grave . . . it's not I who am the Emperor of Rome; it is you who are the Emperor of Rome.

MARCUS What do you mean? I fail to catch the drift.

FRONTO We have already enjoyed here a little play and dance. Now let me tell you a story one of the great poets tells. See! Here is the Old Man of the Sea riding along on the neck of a poor fisherman. It is hot and dry and dusty. The Old Man of the Sea is wise, merciful, considerate; he sees that his mount is tired and in pain. "Stand, stand a moment, fellow," he says, "rest, don't exert yourself so. The sweat's in your eyes; here, let me wipe your brow. Why don't you take a drink of water? We have lots of time. Ah, your feet hurt—you should get better shoes. We'll see to that." He will do everything for him, everything except one thing: he doesn't get down off his back!

MARCUS It's a pleasant story, and I catch the drift. Haven't we often talked about this before? Fronto, we are the servants of the order of the world. Here we are cast. It was not I who made me Emperor of Rome and put this purple on me, heavy to wear. It was my father the pious Antoninus and great Hadrian, and Trajan before that, and first divine Augustus and Julius, to bring back peace into the wrecked world. You know the history of it better than I do. What shall I do except act out my part?

FRONTO (*Impatiently*) Excuse me, I have looked at the order of the world, as you call it. I have looked at it out of the corner of my eye. I have sometimes frankly looked it in the face. All right, give in to it! Here she is!

　　(*The door atop the steps opens.* FAUSTINA *appears, simply dressed*)

85

FAUSTINA   My lord.

MARCUS   Annia Faustina. (*To the others*) Leave us.
(*They go slowly; and she more slowly descends as*
MARCUS *says*)
How like the rational immortal sphere
westering and the equable Scales
and she who holds the Scales sinking low—
while the last outpost of the camp, all night
I wearily watched yonder the enemy—
until the Scales rested on the earth,
middle of April at the crack of Dawn—
so you step off the last step.

                              Come nearer.

FAUSTINA
I am afraid to. You must come to me.

MARCUS
I am not offended with you, Annia Faustina.

FAUSTINA
No, but I am offended with myself.
(*In this scene the actress of* FAUSTINA *must accomplish two things: On the one hand her words, fits, tirades and self-judgments are genuine; on the other hand she is maneuvering* MARCUS *to a decision clear in her own mind*)
You say that you are not offended with me.
I know you are not; for you are perfected
in philosophic apathy. I can
no more offend you than earthquakes o' the earth
or floods or stupidity or envy
or the importunity of idiots
or the malaria that racks you: toward

86

us all you have learned equanimity.
Great gods, *you* are less distant, let me call
on you!

MARCUS

       Annia,
are you offended I am not offended?
Are you jealous of the truth of my life
and wish to make me less to have me more?
Do not be jealous of the stoic truth.
Believe me, I am not offended with you
because my love for Annia Faustina
and my admiration for the mother of my son
and my thanksgiving to the gods for these,
these things are so committed in my soul
that other things are nothing. Not by chance
and not by will alone—although by will—
have I achieved a blessed apathy:
There is an earthly cause, and you are that earthly
      cause.

FAUSTINA

Will you help me, husband, Marcus Aurelius?

MARCUS

Yes, I will help you. What is it to do?

FAUSTINA

First you must kiss away the tears
streaming from my eyes that blind me
and I cannot see your face.
(*He embraces her*)

MARCUS

These are real tears. They taste of salt and pain.
Empress of Rome, do not cry any more.

(*Embracing her, he speaks about himself across her shoulder*)
What I am feeling is a common feeling:
this is strange. Let me lapse into this.
(*He breaks away*)
I dare not, I am not yet prepared
to feel the ordinary without fright.
It rises and it takes me by the throat.
(*They sit on the steps. She says eagerly and cheerfully*)

FAUSTINA Philosopher! Let us make an hypothesis—is that the word you use for supposing?

MARCUS (*Smiling*) Yes, that is the word.

FAUSTINA Supposing there were a person, gifted by fortune—

MARCUS What a pleasure it is to see Annia Faustina frowning and wrinkling her nose again as we used!

FAUSTINA No, listen to what I say.

MARCUS All right. I'll frown too.

FAUSTINA (*With mounting intensity*) Supposing a person, gifted by fortune—I mean with health, wealth, and every pleasure; and thereby exempted from desire for the impossible; and also stationed as even to be exempted from ambition—supposing such a person to be intelligent and learned and instructed by precept and example, and she—or he, it makes no difference—is convinced of all the theorems and commonplaces of philosophy and therefore wishes to live nobly, and to be at peace in the cosmos; nay, more than wishes it, *wills* it, wills to be at peace—

MARCUS   Annia! You are describing a most beautiful, happy person!

FAUSTINA   No! Nevertheless! This person performs and continues to perform, and apparently cannot not perform, such things as produce slavery and misery and turn the cosmos into chaos!

MARCUS   (*Sharply*)   That is impossible. The hypothesis is contradictory—impermissible.

FAUSTINA   No! No! Supposing it! Supposing it! She is detroying herself.

MARCUS   But you *cannot* suppose it if it is self-contradictory. This is logic, Annia. In one part of the hypothesis you deny all grounds of the thing, and in the other part you affirm the thing itself. This is like beginning by saying, "Suppose an eagle is *not* an eagle—" From a contradiction anything whatever follows, or nothing whatever follows. It makes no sense. "Suppose an eagle is not an eagle—therefore Cicero has red hair." Ridiculous!

FAUSTINA   Is it ridiculous? All right, say it is my woman's whim to suppose something ridiculous! Let us *therefore* suppose it.

MARCUS   Annia! Don't be absurd. We cannot use words as if they were guttural noises. This reduces us to the level of the beasts.

FAUSTINA   (*Dreamily*)   Ah! If it is a contradiction, you say, then *anything* follows from it—anything whatever? I like this thought. Let us affirm this contradiction and see what *is* anything whatever. Here is this *fortunate* person, *willing* to be at peace; and day by day is plunged into chaos, and, yes, is taking leave of human senses—reduced to the level of the beasts—roaring, crying out! You yourself have defined it!

MARCUS (*Very troubled*) Stop! Not another word! I refuse to speak of the impossible.

FAUSTINA (*Softly*) Impossible? Is it impossible? Marcus, the impossible is a fact. *I* am such a person.

MARCUS You? Ah, I thought it was myself. And maybe it is every man in Rome. You have cast me in dismay. Why do I wrangle against Fronto—stubbornly—when in the bottom of my heart I am afraid?

FAUSTINA "It is the nature of a reasonable creature," said Marcus Aurelius to himself, "to yield not to any lust or motion of the flesh. For it is part and privilege of the intellective and reasonable faculty that she can so bound herself that neither sense nor lust can prevail. For both these things are brutish. Reason challenges the victory! She cannot endure to be subjected. By nature she is ordained to command!" See, I know the text by heart. Teacher, what shall I do with this *un*reasonable creature?

MARCUS You are not unreasonable, Annia. It is something you tell yourself.

FAUSTINA (*Chanting*)
> Father, save me, I have been
> poisoned. A witch
> is daily drop by drop
> brewing a black elixir: I
> *I* am the witch, there are no other witches.

MARCUS In god's name, hush! How can we converse if you begin to chant fables and images?

FAUSTINA

    Who is beating drums?
It is heartbeats. True!
There are no other gods.
Why do I not sit quiet
in the center of the world?
Now Rome shall sit at peace!
And cross my fingers so.
Come hither, all my sons—
Ahhhhh . . .
*(She emits a long moan and then stands staring, and
then begins to tremble.* MARCUS *shakes her roughly)*

MARCUS

    Come to yourself!

FAUSTINA

                Why, I am still myself.

MARCUS

    I am lost. I understand what has a meaning,
but if I ask it, you will sigh again.
Annia, let us move ourselves awhile
from pestilential Rome, or else move him.

FAUSTINA

    No! for my soul is rising on the couch
shouting at night, "Desire! desire! desire!"
I said, "Give way, my soul, to love,"
I said another time, "To hate give way."
"Adore this! for this is your master." "Oh,
spit your contempt on this obscene slave!"
One day I was degraded by him
and I degraded him another day.

91

I mocked, esteemed, and simply pitied him;
I hated, scorned, and simply pitied me.
Can absence heal the sick imagination
that burns at night when everything is absent?
Can you instruct the imagination with
excellent reasons? O teach them to me!
Let wisdom help me now! Or must I die?
For I will not endure this thing again.

MARCUS (*Quietly*)
This is strange. And also this is common.
I know that there are strange things that are com-
    mon.
There are no witches, Annia, you are right;
yet there are gods unknown, dark powers, devils,
incubi, maybe dreams—I don't know what—
that haunt the imagination in between
the serviceable senses and the will
and procreate themselves and soon are many;
and we fall prey to them, yes, even we,
and reason fails, and the will is weak.
These things I admit are hard for me to admit.
What I shall do is hard for me to do.
Boy!
(*The* MESSENGER *appears*)
    Summon the necromancer, the hag Isis—
say that the Emperor, yes, Marcus Aurelius,
bids her come here. Yes, say this to her:
"Marcus Aurelius, the philosopher!"
And take the ring, or she will disbelieve it.
And—boy!
You may speak it abroad that this is so,

in order that my private shame may be
my public shame.
(MESSENGER *goes out but at once there is a clamor
and he returns*)

MESSENGER   The hag Isis is in the courtyard, shrieking to
be let in.

MARCUS (*Coldly to* FAUSTINA)   What, did *you* call her?

FAUSTINA   I summoned her because I knew you would.

MARCUS (*After a pause*)   Let her come in.
(*Enter* ISIS, *stormily, old, with a cane; tricked out
and ragged, etc., her* BOY *ragged. She is confused and
very grand*)

ISIS   Pray to your gods! On your knees! Pray to your gods—
any old gods; kneeling, that's what does it. From kneeling comes reverence and from reverence religion. All the
ideas are mythology—no harm in it. He dreams up his
myth and she hers. Bring on the table! That's my myth.
(*She calls off stage*) Hiya, garbage! I said they'd let me
in; go home and have a cramp and think of Isis. The
table! The Jews believe in wind when they kneel; the
Egyptians have a god that's a dog. But these folks are intellectuals, I don't need to give them the four-bit lecture.
Here, table, this way! (*To* FAUSTINA) Which is the exact
navel of the room?

FAUSTINA (*Decisively, indicating with her big toe*)   Here is
the exact navel of the room. The umbilical is cut.

ISIS   How the devil did you know that? Put the table here,
and re-establish contact. The Empress of whatsis?

BOY   Rome.

ISIS   The Empress of Rome wants to have her fortune told.
I'll read the Egyptian cards. There's no sure book but a
man's liver, but once that's out of him there's nothing
left to guess about, so we'll use the cards. Where in hell
are the cards? (*She fumbles for the cards in her purse.
Complete disorder ensues—cards fly about; when she
stuffs them back she drops the cane and other things;
and during this comic routine talks imperturbably on*)
The cards—oops, the cards. Contact! Under the table.
You know what I mean, dearie? Cards. Drat. Pray to your
cards and re-establish *reeal* contact. (*Mimicking*) Fronto!
What must I ask myself? Say, "Isn't this really stinking
weather? I mean, this is *real* Italian weather, isn't it?"
You know what I mean by "real," boy?

BOY   (*As if humoring her*)   Sure.

ISIS   I don't. Hee hee. (MARCUS *laughs*) What are *you*
cackling about, peanut?

MARCUS   (*Gravely*)   Why, I thought that was a good joke.

ISIS   Hee hee. I thought so too. (*Angrily*) On your knees!
I said pray to your gods. Down on your knees. Any old
gods. If you don't, it's hopeless. *Down!*

MARCUS   What, must I really kneel and pray?

ISIS   If I say so. Pray and establish contact. Where else is
the power to come from? I haven't got it. I'm a poor tired
thing. It's a lot of shit, but that's how we do it. You too,
madam!

(After a moment MARCUS *falls to his knees; and when he begins to pray,* FAUSTINA *falls to her knees)*

MARCUS   Cosmos, and Capitoline Jupiter, and Remus, and Divine Julius and Augustus, and my father, and you who brought me up: May I will what I will, with a continuous and even energy; for to will something has regard to it, but to will to will it has regard to myself. Grant me what I will to will for, the philosophic apathy: to be undisturbed and act. Whatsoever is material soon vanishes away into the common substance of this whole; and whatsoever is formal is soon resumed into the common reason of the whole; and the fame and memory of everything is soon swallowed up by the general age and duration of the whole.
    (Pause)

FAUSTINA   *(Frightened)*   I do not know what to pray for without falsification. I shall pray this prayer: Chaos! and three-faced witch! and goddess with a Babylonian name! And my mother Annia Galeria! May I, assuming a contradiction, say by a woman's whim, come to experience anything whatever, or nothing whatever, as it follows, it makes no difference. Only, because I hate each idea as it forms in my sick imagination, grant me to know the original violence, before the creation of the heavens and the earth. And at the same time to be avenged! Oh, my sick head!
    *(*ISIS *comes between them and falls to her knees)*

ISIS   Creator spirit, Hermes, and you Leader of the Muses, once more! once more! once more to the saying! although my voice is grown tired and impatient. *(She rises)* Em-

95

press of Rome, now cross my palm with silver. (FAUSTINA
gives her a gold piece) Filth! It's yellow! (*She flings the
coin on the ground, whence, after a moment, a* SOLDIER
picks it up and pockets it)

Do you think I ply this lousy trade for gold?
Only enough for me and the boy to live.
We travel lightly, but we travel wide.
There are other places in the world than Rome,
although you preen yourselves. Now give me silver.
(FAUSTINA *gives her silver*)
Take the eighth card and lay it face up, here.
Here is the present, here is past, and here
is future. This is the leading card of your life.
(*Holding up the tarot card*)
Why, it is *Temperance*! See how she pours the stream
free, fearless, accurate from jug to jug
and does not lose a drop. She has wings,
but as yet she lightly stands on the ground
like a dancer. And a jewel on her forehead.
Madam, you have been lying to yourself,
the cards do not lie.

Give me another card
and see what you negate: *the Wheel of Chance*.
Madam, you were not made to rise and fall
and whirl and hope and fall, like these bound beasts
with the dizzy look as if they were listening.
That's past and done with and will be no more.
Give me: *the Juggler!* That's my card, not yours.
It means you are secure in my hands.
I'll choose the next. Owaii! *The six of Hearts!*
So, and what's this? Hmm. Is that the way?
Pick me another one, a little one.

(*She whistles and pauses, musing.* FAUSTINA *takes another card and* ISIS, *laying it on the table, exclaims*)
All red? All? All?

FAUSTINA

For god's sake, mother, what does it mean?

ISIS

Hush, madam, give! give! give!
I'm seeing here what we'll not see the end of.
It's not every day I read the cards of Rome.
(MARCUS *rises from his knees*)
More! more! Aha! aha! I've seen enough.
(*She scatters cards and overturns the table*)
My head is roaring with a mighty thing
I could announce and make the walls fall down.
(*The* BOY *cautions her with a finger to his lips*)
Never fear, child, I do not counsel kings.
Nor would he ask me, would you?

MARCUS

No, I would not.

ISIS (*To* FAUSTINA, *very reasonably and more and more confidentially*) As for your case, madam, I have the answer to it. But hard thinking would itself have given this answer, without consulting an Egyptian book.

FAUSTINA   I cannot think, tell me what I must do.

ISIS   Come closer, you two, and I'll explain what you must do. What is the case? The case is this: A woman suffers from a diseased imagination. Her mind is haunted by pictures and the pictures call up desire, and contrariwise the desire calls up the pictures. She does what she doesn't

97

want to do, or she struggles against it and goes out of her mind. Is that it?

FAUSTINA That's nearly it.

ISIS Now you children, you can't control the imagination by will and you can't control it by reasons. You will and still it burns, and you make reasons and the imagination invents other reasons, according to desire. It comes upon you! It blows like fire! You can't control him from outside, by jails; or by going away; or by acting out; or by not acting out. There he is still, terrible, terrible. And the worst of all the imaginations are these lusts, because lust is close to nature itself—

FAUSTINA Oh, come to the point.

ISIS (*Angrily*) I'll come to it soon enough! The point! The point! (*Wildly*) Kill the gladiator! Kill him! That's the point—everybody knows *that*. But will he *stay* dead? Existing in your dreams, destroying the future, too, with resentment and remorse, and shrieking nightmares at two o'clock in the morning. (*They face away from her*) I'll come to the point soon enough, Your Highness. What in the devil do you take me for? And what do you two take yourselves for? You have been living with yourself for forty years, and can't you hear me out for ten minutes?

MARCUS Listen to her, Annia. Speak, mother.

ISIS These lusts—they are continually renewed. You can't rely even on time for relief, time that consoles mourning for the dead. I have known men to make fools of themselves the same way every day for half a century! Time! Space! Will! Reason! All are hopeless. We have to use stronger measures.

FAUSTINA   Ah! I think so, too. Tell me, what must I do?

ISIS   The imagination, madam, may be quieted by setting
up a counterimagination. Not a reason, not a prison, but
a present memory. Fire with fire! Let us look into this.
What is it? What is it in the imagination that is the contrary of lust? Lady?

FAUSTINA   I don't know what it is, I can't imagine.

ISIS   Lady, the opposite of lust is *horror*! In lust the flesh
rises and creeps outward; in horror it shrinks inward and
the hairs stand on end. Do you follow me? Horror is the
power to establish. And how can we make this exist in
your imagination? Therefore, what you must do, what I
advise you to do, is this—

> (*Her voice has been sinking to a whisper and trails
> off as they walk slowly away*)

Curtain

ACT TWO

*The scene is the hall of the first act, but closed in: a gold
curtain across the back, the steps and the door gone, the
front lower exit stopped. It is the soul of FAUSTINA with no
bodily opening, but of course there is always the proscenium
opening, the absent fourth wall. As the scene develops, the
posture and positions of the actors are to suggest a Byzantine fixity. The play is, in one aspect, the freezing of the
philosophic man into the Byzantine Emperor.* MARCUS
AURELIUS *and* FAUSTINA *are disclosed on thrones, in ceremonial robes. But their crowns are on the table. He sits on
the right of the stage and moves about as he speaks. But
she, against the golden backdrop, to the right, stares forward, motionless.*

MARCUS (*Seated, picking up the crown*) Asia, Europe.
What are they? They are small corners of the whole flat
world. The Great Sea is a drop of water in the ocean.
Towering Mount Atlas is only a clod of dirt. The present
moment—the present moment is one little point of
eternity. All! Petty things—things that are soon changed,
soon perished. Do you understand that, Annia? (*She
stares forward silently.* MARCUS *rises and moves, laying
down the crown*) Annia Faustina! Consider it this way:
Would a person, would you, choose to live it over again?
I say to myself, "What! to see the things of the world
again, as I have already seen them? Public ceremonials,
pompously empty. Stage plays! People like herds of cattle.
Conflicts, rubbing one another the wrong way. A bone
thrown to a crowd of hungry dogs; a bait for greedy fishes.
Wretched ants painfully dragging their burdens. Fright-

ened mice running to and fro. Puppets pulled up and down by wires and nerves. There are the objects of the world!" Would you live this again, Annia? (*She is silent*) Wake up! wake up, Annia, out of your natural dream! Stir your wits. Look! Now when you are quite awake, you see that these are only dreams that trouble you, just as man awakes from night sleep, terrified and sweating, and he sees that it was only a dream. (*She turns away her head. In anguish*) How are we to live, Annia? What is it like? Is it like dancing? No. The art of living in this world is like the art of wrestling, to learn to be ready wherever it comes; and to learn not to be pinned down.

> (ROMANS *enter, not marching but formally. At most, five or six of them.* MARCUS *seats himself and puts on his crown*)

FAUSTINA   Who are these people? Must it be public before them?

MARCUS   So it must be. As I am Marcus, I am a citizen of Rome—and these are Romans. As I am a man, I am a citizen of the universe. Is not Rome a good sample of all the universe there is?

FAUSTINA   This hall is shut in. There used to be doors and windows here.

MARCUS   Yes, it is shut in at last. Now we must engender miracles out of our own guts.

ROMANS IN CHORUS

> Marcus Aurelius and Annia Faustina,
> Lord and Lady of the ordered world,
> stand up! Your robes are stiff
> and will keep you from falling down.
> (*They stand*)

MARCUS

Put on your crown.

FAUSTINA

Must I put on this crown?

ROMANS IN CHORUS

Put on your crown, Annia Faustina,
and hold up the sky over my head.
Gold does not rust. O brothers!
Open your startled eyes.
(*They stand symmetrically on either side of the Empress looking slightly toward her, in the pattern of the Byzantine group. She puts on her crown and assumes the formal smile*)
The smile of the Empress of Rome
is neither benevolent nor malevolent.
I am surprised into immobility—
only my eyes are alive.

MARCUS   If this pose were not natural it could not endure. How long can these things endure?

ROMAN SPOKESMAN   Your Majesty, what have we come to watch? My eyes have learned to be startled while my face remains impassive.

MARCUS   A public ritual. Our suffering is a public ritual. It is not the case, my children, that your parents do not suffer and suffer passion. You hear the rumor of it. We may not hide and grieve in secrecy. All Rome must bear us witness and cry out.

SPOKESMAN   Ah, may we cry out? What must we cry out?

MARCUS   You may cry, "Ow!"

ROMAN CHORUS   *Ow!*

MARCUS   No, it is not yet time.

ROMAN CHORUS (*In whisper*)
>   She is still smiling.
>   How terrible
>   is the suffering of the Empress!
>   How long can these things endure?

MARCUS   Let the ritual begin.
>   (A *pause. In silence the* BOY *brings in the table and places it as before. In silence he brings a silver bowl and a large knife and places them on the floor. He begins to sharpen the knife. The chorus stirs*)

SPOKESMAN   Your Majesty, what are these preparations? They are not beautiful.

MARCUS   It will become clear.

SPOKESMAN   No, we have the right to know.

MARCUS   Hush, here is the priestess herself.
>   (*The* BOY *plays a piercing phrase on a pipe again and again.* ISIS *appears in a black robe—she is a crazy old woman*)

ISIS   Bring on the act of horror! Bursting inside me, let us act it out. Aiiii-i-iii-aiii— (*She staggers to the table and presides behind it, supporting herself*) So. Good evening, horror. Well met in Rome. Here they are frozen into immobility and they look with startled eyes. What are you staring at if you do not cry out?

SPOKESMAN   It is not yet time to cry out.

ISIS   No, this is the time! this is the time! Afterwards it is too late. The horror is the immobility. Look, this people is corroding away (*She pokes at a* ROMAN)— it flakes off.

And they imagine they are made of gold. Where is the victim for the slaughter? I remember that I was to kill a man. (*She approaches* MARCUS *with the knife*) Is it you?

MARCUS No, madam, it is not I.

ISIS Naturally it's not you. You philosopher. You Emperor. Naturally it's always the youngest and potent of the tribe, some bully boy apt at fucking; he's the one to have his throat cut—to bleed—to bleed. Now it comes back to me—you, the Empress Faustina—this is Rome, isn't it Rome, Boy?

BOY Yes, Rome.

ISIS The daughter of Annia Galeria, what more need I say! (*She cackles*) By the way, may I mention it in all this company?

MARCUS You are supposed to mention everything that concerns me before the people of Rome.

ISIS Well, this Faustina—who is standing there grinning—this Empress has got herself hot in the pants for a slave, a gladiator. Burning, my dearies. Standing out o' bed in the dead o' night and shouting. But what! Instead of being happy like another woman that she has at least this bit of contact, such as it is, with the meaning of life—no, she has become vindictive because the mistress of Rome is not the mistress of herself. These are the customs of Rome. So they have called on Isis for help.

SPOKESMAN Marcus Aurelius, must we listen to this and not put our cloaks over our heads and look the other way?

MARCUS No, you must listen to it patiently.

SPOKESMAN (*To the others*) Listen, lewd ears.

ISIS   And I say, I, Isis, "Horror! Horror can cure the sick imagination. I'll cut this bully's throat and let the blood of it pour over milady—it spurts and comes cascading down in a sheet over her pale body. *Then* she won't think of him with pleasure any more; but if she comes to think of him, her bristles will stand on end and she'll shrink inward. Tomorrow, mark my words, she won't think of him at all. Forgotten. No more. And her smile will be as frigid as a piece of ice." (*Brandishing the knife*) That's it. Where's the strong boy? Let's get on, get on!

SPOKESMAN   Is this true, what she says?

MARCUS   Yes, all true. These are the sufferings of my family and you have come to bear witness.

SPOKESMAN   Of your family? Pardon me, Your Majesty, but it seems to me that it is the gladiator who will suffer the most.

MARCUS   We are all members of one another, and the suffering of one is the suffering of another.

ISIS   (*Banging crazily on the bowl with the knife*) Too much talk! Bang! Dong! Ashmodee. Abracadabra and all that shit. Aiiiii! Aii! (*Suspicious whispering*) We are being watched. Strangers are looking at us, enemies. (*She walks to the proscenium opening and begins to explore it with her hands as though it were glass*) What's this wall? Here is an invisible wall. It seems to be open, but they cannot come through here. No one can enter here and take part.

Holy Spirit! then what's the use of it?

Must I shed the blood of a shrieking boy for a show?

A show, an entertainment, a thrill?

Re-enacting the old legends of old Rome
like a storyteller—and they will not move.
They will not move but sit with startled eyes.
They will not come and beat the ground in rhythm
and circle round the altar and cry out,
and give themselves once more to springtime life.
What is the use of murder
if the animal spirits do not flow again?
We are *already* fixed in horror, Boy,
the horror is the immobility.
(*She bursts into tears and flings herself down on the
table weeping. The* BOY *blows hopelessly on the pipe.
A screen is brought in and set up, concealing the
table and* ISIS. MARCUS *holds out his fist and it has
turned to gold. He stares at it impassively a moment*)

MARCUS The Roman Emperor has a golden fist. (*He
pounds on the floor with this fist; the sound of a hammer*) Where are my teachers Fronto and the old mother
Cornelia? I said that they were not to be spared their
presence.

SOLDIER They will not come. Must they be dragged by
force?

MARCUS By force. (*Exit* SOLDIER) Through the substance
of the universe as through a torrent pass all particular
bodies. How many such as Socrates, how many such as
Plato, how many such as Epictetus hath the age of the
world long since swallowed up and devoured! Let this
come to my mind when my thoughts are too distracted
by the present or are set too earnestly about their business.
Of all my thoughts and cares, one only thing shall be
the object: that I myself do nothing contrary to the

proper constitution of a man. (*Passionate*) Oh, the time when I shall have forgotten all things is at hand, and the time also is at hand when I shall be forgotten by all things. (*Quietly*) There is nothing that is new. All things that are, are usual; nor do they last long.

(*Enter* FRONTO *and* CORNELIA, *dragged*)

FRONTO So. I have come after all. (*To* SOLDIER) Thank you.

SOLDIER Thank me? I apologized for laying hands on you, old man, you need not be sarcastic. I do my duty, like everyone at the court, including the Emperor.

FRONTO No, no, sincerely, thank you! You have taught me something. You have proved something very valuable for me to know.

SOLDIER Proved something? What have I proved to you?

FRONTO You have proved that you are stronger than I. So, let us look about at this court, it is a fascinating study. Once upon a time there was a cataclysm of violence and here you see the end-products of the violence. Where they fell after the explosion. Congealed with fright— staring with startled eyes. They can't scream. They can't run away. Say, you, why don't you scream and take to your heels? Isn't that the instinctive reaction? What are you staring at? What's there further to see? I seem to belong to the olden times. Curst the day that I began to survive into this present generation! Hey, what's this? The Emperor has grown a golden fist. This is something new —I am surprised. I do not have the stoic apathy. Here, let me look. (MARCUS *holds out the fist and* FRONTO *examines it*) Hmm. Interesting. Can you feel with that? Let me try a pin. Can you touch, finger something, take and give, shake hands? Could you caress a woman with that?

MARCUS No, I can only pound, like a hammer. (*Pounds*) And maybe *grip*—but not let go again. I am afraid to try it.

FRONTO Is this good?

MARCUS I don't know. It is so.

FRONTO Aurelius?

MARCUS My teacher?

FRONTO Why have you brought me here? There are preparations for a brutal act. Didn't I warn you rather to transport this gladiator far away, before you dealt out a worse vengeance? Now what advantage is it, to me, to you, for me to see a horror?

MARCUS Much advantage, to me. It is essential for you to be present.

FRONTO Why is it essential?

MARCUS In order that I may test myself step by step, as I proceed. It is essential for me to be right—it is essential for me to prove to myself that I am right. That is how I am. I say to myself: "Look in the eyes of Fronto and see if your gaze will flinch. Listen to what he says and answer him rejoinder for rejoinder." My gaze will not flinch and I shall have an answer.

FRONTO Immortal gods! If I believed in the gods. How simple the matter is and how complicated he makes it! The man is insanely jealous; a gladiator is embracing his wife's body—and this is important to him, why, I know not. But he does not dare picture to himself this fact, this simple fact. Instead he invents reasons and ceremonials. What a great to-do about a little thing!

MARCUS Is it a little thing to kill a man? In order to do it I must explain many things to myself. Yes, and all Rome must bear me witness; and also Fronto. How am I to live with myself if I am not step by step justified. Tell me, on what grounds would you kill the man?

FRONTO I? I should not kill him. In the first place I would not be enraged, for Annia Faustina is the daughter of Annia Galeria. But if I were in fact jealous and enraged, I would send him away and let my jealousy rage itself out. Or suppose I were young and my blood was hot, then I would have killed him on the instant and let my anger rage itself out. Where in this must I have grounds and justification?

MARCUS You see, the men of that time gave in to their passions. Lucky for them. But I must try to be perfect and do what is reasonable. I cannot raise my hand unless I am justified. You see this golden grip. What shall I grip with it? The first thing I shall grip is the wrist of my other hand. Now I shall not strike, until I know perfectly. A chief of state is not like another man.

FRONTO Not like a man? Enough! The man is driven. Did you say Perfect, Marcus? Did you use this word? Then I'll hear nothing more and say nothing more. I am too real to be a character in your bad dream, Marcus, even if I am a Roman citizen.

(*He turns away*)

MARCUS Teacher—

FRONTO   No. No more.
(*He shakes his head and covers his ears*)

MARCUS   You say that I am jealous. That's true. Hear it, Romans: what he says is true. But there is something more than that. But I do not know what it is. Teacher, explain it.
(FRONTO *stubbornly shakes his head and goes to the other corner*)

MARCUS   This is unkindly, Fronto. I am disappointed. Well, it was not I who failed to give the last rejoinder. Where is the next I must reduce to silence?
(*He looks down and sees that he is still gripping his wrist. He relaxes the grip and makes a sign. Pause.* SOLDIERS *enter with* GALBA, *chained*)

GALBA   (*Confused*)   I don't understand. Do you understand? I'll be late. Let me go, I tell you I'll be late. He said, "Set that man free!"—myself. It was the other one, there—no, not you, other soldiers—fell on me and pinned my arms. But Marcus Aurelius said, "Set that man free!" In ringing tones; he is the Emperor! And the soldiers fell back from me at once. And then he said, "Let him go free in Rome. Tomorrow he will fight in the arena, if he so pleases." You may suppose that I haven't forgotten a single one of those words; the ringing tones of it are ringing still in my ears. Well, it does so please me to fight in the arena! And today I am not going to turn the sword, although I *did* use to turn it. Why am I in chains, as if *I* were the bear dragged up from the cellar to be let loose on the sand? The crowd is gathering—what am I doing here? There he is! My Emperor! Marcus! Marcus Aurelius!

MARCUS I hear you, boy. You need not shout so loud. Speak in your ordinary tone.

GALBA Tell them to set me free, say it again, that I may hear the words a second time.

MARCUS That is not your ordinary tone. Listen to your voice. We want to speak earnestly and reasonably.

GALBA (*Lowering his voice, but soon beginning to stutter*) But—but I am in these chains. The c-crowd is collecting. I do not want to be late, Your Majesty. L-late. L-l-l-late.

MARCUS There will be no fights in the arena today. You see, all Rome is here. You are not late.

GALBA (*Relieved*) No fights today? And I'm not late. Oh, then it makes no difference. Thank you. What must we talk about? You hear, I am speaking in my ordinary tone. This is very interesting—I never listened to my own voice before. It does not sound like I thought. It is—frightened. Why am I in chains?

MARCUS You must not say, "*It* is frightened," as if it were not your voice. You must say, "*I* am frightened and it sounds in my voice."

GALBA *I* am frightened—why am I in chains? No, I am beginning to talk loud again.

MARCUS Gladiator! If you keep listening only to your voice, you won't pay any attention to what we say; but you must pay strict attention.

GALBA Yes, I'll pay strict attention; I am sorry. But if I try to speak in my ordinary voice—then s-s-suddenly I f-f-feel these heavy chains on my shoulders and I can't pay attention to anything else. How is that? (*Loudly*) Tell them to let me out of the chains so that I can pay strict attention to what we say. Ah!

MARCUS What are you staring at?

GALBA Your fist. You have a golden fist.

MARCUS Child, you must prepare to die.

GALBA Die? (*Pause*) I'm not old—young—it's not likely—oh, I understand! Anyone is likely to die all of a sudden. The plague carries you off in the dog days. Or—especially in the arena? Is that what you mean—a man in my profession? Yes, I ought to think of this—instead of just living right on from morning to night and again from morning to night, right on, right on—a friend—
    (*He pauses*)

MARCUS You were saying, a friend?

GALBA A close friend of mine died in the arena last week ... How throaty my voice is.

MARCUS (*Tired*) Gladiator, if you keep listening to your voice—if you keep staring at my hand—how can we speak seriously? Here, I'll hold this hand behind my back.

GALBA That's better. I'm sorry, Your Majesty, you make me self-conscious, first about my voice, then about my staring. And now my teeth are chattering. These chains— Galba! Take hold of yourself—pay attention! You were saying? Prepare to die—

MARCUS Consider it, young man: Death is a cessation from the impressions of the senses, from the tyranny of the passions, from the errors of the mind, and from the slavery of the body.

GALBA Repeat that more slowly, I can't take it in. I only began to be wise yesterday. Death is a cessation—stop, that means stop, doesn't it? Death is a stop. What are—impressions?

MARCUS Yes, it's a stop. By impressions I mean what you see and hear—the lights and shadows you see, the sounds you hear, all stopped. No more staring in fright, no more listening anxiously for a footstep.

GALBA I understand. Death is like—black and still. That's easy. And what was the next thing stopped? You said three and four.

MARCUS Death stops the tyranny of the passions. The passions are anger, hatred, envy, and lust, and longing, and ambition—

GALBA Stopped. You mean a dead man doesn't try to win any more, and doesn't fly into a rage when he loses—

MARCUS No more fear, and no more feeling guilty. No more ambition to be always right.

GALBA (*Manly, face to face*) Why—are you so hot to die, Marcus Aurelius? What's the matter, father? Is there a help for it?
(*Brief pause*)

MARCUS Do you care for this, that I am troubled, and maybe want to die?

GALBA Yes, I care for you.

MARCUS I care for you, Galba.

GALBA This is the second time you told me so.

MARCUS Then see! what difference does it make what I care or you care? Death is what it is. Everything is what it is.

GALBA (*Notices* FAUSTINA *smiling in the group*) Annia! Ah, is that the Empress? I never saw her with a crown— and now—how still they are, I thought it was a picture— I would not touch her. This is not my type. I'm sorry— A dead man—a dead man, Your Majesty, doesn't have any sexual desire. I understand that. Sir, is that good? I mean, not to see or hear, not to have sexual pleasure, nor even to fly in a rage. Oh! I'd have to think about that. To me it's a new thought. Might we speak of it some other time? These chains are uncomfortable, you have to hold your hand behind your back. I mean, some other time when both of us are feeling more at ease. Your Majesty, tell them to strike off these chains.

MARCUS If you were dead, you wouldn't feel the chains.

GALBA (*Flat*) No.

MARCUS (*Urgent*) Gladiator! It's hard to be reasonable. You'll find that it's impossible to put these things off to a further time; it is now we must discuss them. But you young men—may I speak as an older man?—you young men are so strongly attached to your sexual pleasures, and to flying in rages, as if that were the Good itself. And always wanting to be comfortable! Then how is it possible to govern the Republic? And yet, wherever I turn, everybody is like that.

GALBA (*Suddenly notices the screen, behind which is* ISIS) What's that screen? . . . Why am I in chains?

MARCUS It is a screen.

GALBA   Was it there? I didn't notice it.

VOICE OF ISIS   Hey! hey! Hurry! hurry!

GALBA   Oh, someone's behind there!

ISIS   Too much talk.
(*She pounds the knife on the bowl*)

GALBA   Why is she there? What is she saying?

ISIS   Bang! Dong! Dang! Bing!
(*Banging away*)

GALBA   Why is she doing that?

MARCUS   I'm afraid she's a little crazy.
(*Silence. Pause*)

GALBA   *I'm* afraid. Why am I afraid? What's that screen? Marcus Aurelius! You say, "Everybody—all the young people are like that." Are you talking about *all* the young men who hunt for love and quarrel? You aren't pointing it especially at me, are you? I offended you.

MARCUS   No, everybody. But you're a part of everybody, aren't you?

GALBA   But why am *I* in chains? That's what I want to know. (*Wandering suddenly*) Was there a day when I was *not* in chains?

MARCUS   Galba, Galba—you're like a child. When I'm trying to talk about the highest matters, you keep harping on a small discomfort. You mustn't lose the track—

GALBA   No! What's that screen? Why am I afraid? *Who* is there? *Am* I in chains? They're in chains! Look, all of them are in chains! Annia! Why are you in chains? Annia, wait, wait a while for me, I'm coming.

MARCUS (*Warning*)   Galba!

GALBA   There must have been a time when I was not in chains! (*Defeated*) I mustn't lose track. If I were dead— if I were dead I wouldn't feel the chains. . . oh.
(*He staggers and makes as if to say "I," but cannot utter a sound and stands gagging*)

MARCUS   What's wrong? Are you thinking of your dead friend again?

GALBA   No. Ex-x-cuse me. For a m-m-moment it seemed— black. (*Pause*) The id-d-dea you m-mention—

MARCUS   Speak slower and you won't stammer.

GALBA (*Slowly*)   The idea you mention, "If—if I were dead"—I find it hard to imagine that idea. Is that what you mean, it's hard to be reasonable? In order to be reasonable— (*A pause. He cannot speak, and the tears run down his cheeks. If he were not in chains, he would apologize by pointing to his helpless mouth*) In order to be reasonable, must I imagine this idea?

MARCUS (*Simply*)   Yes, I think so. How can we talk seriously about things in general if we don't think of them as applying to ourselves?

GALBA   Ah. (*He is again unable to speak. His teeth are chattering and his knees knocking. No sound except for the knocking of the chains. Tearful*) I'm sorry, sir. But I can't go on for a moment. It'll pass.

MARCUS (*Moved*)   Are you so affected? I can hardly remember what it's like to talk seriously to simple people, who aren't inured to philosophy. Good. While we are waiting, let us summarize. We are speaking about your preparing to die. Now death is a cessation of the sensations, and of the tyranny of the passions. Are you ready to consider the third point, the errors of the mind?

FRONTO (*Advancing*) Stop it! Devil out of hell! Do you want the boy to consent to his own murder?

MARCUS (*Sharply*) If he cannot answer, must he not consent?

FRONTO Free him and he'll answer; not with words, but running away like a live animal.

GALBA What did he say? What did that man say?

FRONTO He's speechless. Do you know why he is speechless? The man is speechless with impotent rage.

MARCUS (*Pounding*) Silence that man! How dares he interrupt the flow of reason?
(*The soldiers lay hands on* FRONTO, *but he bursts into loud laughter*)

GALBA Sir—sir—

MARCUS What are you laughing at?

GALBA Your Majesty—Marcus Aurelius—

FRONTO I'm laughing at how you mistake your tone. You think you're Socrates, but you sound like a sadistic homosexual torturing the love he hates.

MARCUS (*Firmly*) I too know that, you fool. It's true I love him dearly. He cares for me.

GALBA (*Wailing*) Listen to me, father; what did that man say?

MARCUS Be quiet a moment, boy. Is there to be no order in our thoughts. Do you hear it, Romans? It's true what

Fronto says. I am jealous not because of Faustina but because of the gladiator. Even so, there is something more to it than that! Something more. (*Recovering himself*) What is it, boy?

GALBA (*Sober and sharp*) That man said, my murder. Mine! Consent to my own murder. Be honest with me, man: Is this why I am in chains?

MARCUS Yes. I was speaking first of the universal topics, I was concluding to the particular example. This is how we always reason.

GALBA It's I who am to die, not somebody else? Not tomorrow, but today? Father?

MARCUS (*Wild and strange*) Beloved child, you must be persuaded to agree to die. Otherwise all philosophy is a lie. It's not—whatever they think—it's not either the Empress or the gladiator that I'm jealous of—Annia! Annia mother!—no, I am jealous of your pride of life.

> (*He rips away his scarf, disclosing on his breast an emblem. The screen opens, disclosing* ISIS *with the knife. Seeing* ISIS, GALBA *at once begins to bellow and struggle, in the extremity of health fighting for existence*)

GALBA (*As loud as he can*) Help! Help! Help! Help!
> (*He pounds the irons and can hardly be restrained*)

MARCUS Listen to me, moderate your words.

GALBA Help! Help! Help!

MARCUS Gag him, for I must prove it to the end! (*They silence him*) You'd think he had no attachment but to living. Why does he call out this particular word? Is this the spontaneous outcry in such a case?

FRONTO   What would you cry out, in such a case?

MARCUS (*Largamente*)   I am in such a case, and I am crying out. Consider it, wrestler! wrestler in the arena!
(GALBA *is rolling his eyes and struggling, but* MARCUS *pro-
ceeds as though he were indeed listening*) Consider how
it is! The nature of the universe, the common substance
of all things, is like so much wax, and now by chance it
is formed into a horse; and a little later that shape is destroyed and the matter of it is newly formed into the body
of a man; and then next day—today—into some other
form altogether. Is any one so foolish as to fear change,
to which all things that once were not owe their being?
What is more pleasing and familiar in nature? Gladiator!
How could you use the hot baths if the firewood were
not changed and destroyed? How could you eat and be
strong if the food were not destroyed and changed? Don't
you see that for you to come to change by death is a thing
of the very same kind? It is necessary for the universe.

GALBA (*Momentarily ungagged*)   Help!
(*He is silenced*)

MARCUS   He doesn't want to reason about this.

FAUSTINA (*In the group, ceasing to smile*)
What animal sound wakens me from my trance?
How far off those things seem! The men are small.
Alas! how my poor little soul on its
pinnacle of greatness freezing sits!
The animals are roaring in the arena.
There used to be a window here to look from
but now I am shut in and must engender
marvels from my own guts. I am Faustina.
I'll bring forth babes without the aid of men.

Suddenly it is quiet, like the moment
after the wreck.
(*The* BOY *appears from behind the screen*)

BOY (To FAUSTINA)
Your Majesty, excuse me.
You must unassume this magnificence
and be naked.

FAUSTINA

Must I take off this crown?

BOY

Yes, and the robe, although you wear them well.

FAUSTINA
Do I not wear them well! Here, take the crown
and help me out of the robe.

BOY (*Staggering*)

Why, it is heavy.
(*She appears in a white shift*)

FAUSTINA (*Lightly*)
Stiff corset and stiff morals. I am ready.

ROMAN CHORUS
Ought we to look
at the becoming nakedness of the Empress?
But while we are discussing the question
we scrutinize it.

BOY

So come this way.

FAUSTINA

Lead me where I must kneel.

ACT TWO

*(They go behind the screen and it closes. The pipe
sounds low.* GALBA *is still—from the first words of*
FAUSTINA*)*

MARCUS

    He is still. Is his fit of fever past?
    For I have had nights of malaria
    when I imagine only the impossible
    but afterwards the cooler common day breaks.
    Might I speak with him now?

CORNELIA

                    You learned fool!

MARCUS

    Madam, am I a fool?

CORNELIA

              Don't you recognize
    the crafty eyes of a live animal
    because he cannot struggle any more?
    He doesn't want to reason about this,
    he wants to live,
    and then he'll reason among other things.
    Now there is one word that is relevant,
    "Set the man free." Please to say this word.
    (MARCUS *turns away*)
    Marcus, I am not contemptuous of you
    and I am not indignant with the lady
    for I have seen—I have seen nothing else—
    how always! always! always!— *(She stops)*

MARCUS

    Go on. What is it you have always seen?

121

CORNELIA

>I don't remember what I meant to say.
>Always—is it now the time of day
>to bore you with the wisdom of old ladies?

MARCUS

>Damnation! If you have another thought,
>teach me! Do you think I want to stay
>in this narrow collar of my clear ideas
>choking me?

CORNELIA   No, I can't remember it. Maybe I meant to say that you, in your frozen years, can't endure the heat of children; you'd rather murder them. But I'm sure you know this and don't need me to tell you. O my poor child! (*She embraces* GALBA) If I had some food, I'd feed you with it, little son. Romans! I hate the words of war by which you die in far-off places, and the words of peace that kill you here at home. You compliant mothers! I despise you. (*To* GALBA) You're looking at me. You're not darting your eyes about. Let me take off this gag. Soldier, take off this gag, the knot is too tight for me to manage. (*The* SOLDIER *cuts it*) So. May I kiss you, boy?

GALBA   I love you, mother. You make sense. That's why I talk quietly to you and don't scream. It's sweet to talk to you and I want to enjoy this last pleasure. I have not persuaded myself to consent to die, but I see it's useless and painful to struggle. I seem to have shrunk inward, to a quieter place. See, mother, admire me! How wise I have become and how I watch myself. This is really terrible. It's true that fright and horror can stop the rising of desire. I would never have believed it! But here I am not fighting for the only life I have. I could not cry for help if I tried. Yet—this is amazing, an entirely new experience, to talk to you and feel the pleasure of fluent thoughts. Consider this Emperor—his secret is simple. It's simple to me but not to him. He's afraid to die, just like me, but his fright is so overwhelming that he can't even feel it, whereas I, I suppose, got accustomed in the arena. Therefore— (*He laughs*) Really! How I've learned to express myself and say "therefore," just like an educated man! Aren't you proud of me? Because he's afraid, he spends all his life proving that life is worthless and actually longing for change and death, even before it's necessary! And so he dreams up the Universe—what he calls the "substance of the Universe"—to be as permanent and unchanging and immortal as can be, much more so than it is. For something new is always happening, always! (*CORNELIA starts. He yawns. He laughs*) Why do I keep seeing the humorous side? If I had the time I'd think about this too. But (*Yawns*) it wears you out, thinking and following the thoughts. I never got so sleepy wrestling in the arena. Don't mind me, mother, if I fall asleep. Stay here.

    (*He sleeps*)

MARCUS Why, he's asleep.

CORNELIA Yes, he's asleep.

MARCUS This is new. I didn't count on this. Let him go, mother. (*He grips her firmly, but not cruelly, with his golden fist and puts her aside*) Soldier, carry him there and complete the ritual as we planned it. It doesn't mean what I thought it meant, but it means something—that I must do—I am confused. (*They carry sleeping* GALBA *behind the screen*) I am confused. There are many reasons, all true. They are not incompatible, but I don't grasp the common thread. What must I tell myself, being confused? Say this to yourself, "Whatever happens to you, you are by your natural constitution either able to bear it or not able to bear it. Now if you are able, don't be offended, but bear it. But if you are not able, don't be offended either, for it will soon make an end of you, and it itself, whatever it is, will end with you."

ROMAN CHORUS   *Ow.*
  (*They cover their faces*)

FRONTO
   This used to be a human being. Now
   I don't know what it is. But as for me,
   I knew the days when men, when crossed, were angry,
   afraid of hurt, and greedy for pleasure and glory,
   and we used our wits as weapons. We did not
   commit a murder for the idea of it
   nor make love on the counsel of physicians.
   The priesthood took care of the rituals,
   people were not self-conscious; yet we trod
   warier, day by day, than these madmen.
   So it was, if indeed it was,
   but as it is, I cannot live any more.
   (*He falls on his sword and dies*)

MARCUS   Help! (*Chokes*) I can't—I can't cry it out. That's strange. Dying! They're all freezing—into immobility. Not agreed! I'm not agreed to it! Why am I speaking speech in this extremity? The boy spoke out of mother love. (*Firmly and with dignity*) Let me speak meaningful language to the end, and find consolation in the beautiful syntax of it, and so universalize a little this sorry condition of myself. For as I am myself, I am no good to me. So. (*In a normal voice*) Help! If I speak it, I can speak it out.

(*Then, as if remembering a dream*)
During the war in Pannonia,
and the barbarians, the loud Quadi
who wear the claws of panthers in their hats,
came round us more and more, and still they came,
and more and more and more, and we were lost—
in howling darkness—while their eyes flashed. Then
did our legions cry out with one quiet voice,
"Thundering God, grant us, grant us confusion!"
There came a thunderclap. They were confounded.
Hailstones fell from heaven. And they fled.
(*Very quiet and sweet*)
Do you not hear the silver trumpet far?
"Victory! Victory!"
(*He chokes, and coughs, and withdraws rapidly off, in nausea. Rapid, loud, rhythmic pipe and drum. The screen opens, disclosing* FAUSTINA *in a brick-red dress. Immediately the background scene darkens away. And at once* FAUSTINA, *in a spotlight, begins to beat to the rhythm and dances a few motions—large, free, and joyous—unfrozen. But the music breaks off; the spot on* FAUSTINA *rapidly dims; the stage is quite dark except that, in front, are lit two spots on either side of the proscenium shining directly at each other, making a curtain of hardly visible light that, however, bursts into flame when* FAUSTINA's *hands subsequently reach into it*)

FAUSTINA (*In the dimness*) I can't dance. I must break out
of here. There isn't any love in the past. This place is self-
contained, like crazy thoughts. There will be a time, later,
to weep bitterly for the bravery and beauty murdered, and
also for the murderer of beauty and bravery. But now!
now, which way can I go? . . . What is this invisible
wall? Here is the absent fourth wall of this place. (*She
peers through, her face ablaze*) It's dark there.

> (*She turns away.* ISIS *appears beside her and they
> talk in loud whispers*)

ISIS No, daughter! That is the way out! Go through.

FAUSTINA Here? You yourself said that they were enemies.

ISIS They are enemies because there is a boundary. When
you disregard the boundary, they will cease to be enemies.

FAUSTINA But there *is* a boundary. How can I disregard it?
Where does it extend? It goes here—here—here. (*She ex-
plores it with her flaming hands*) Is there no exit?

ISIS There is an obvious exit. Through! go through! You
must no longer act somebody else's play.

FAUSTINA Mother, help me! Push me to be born.

ISIS Impossible! It is too late for that.
> (*She vanishes*)

FAUSTINA (*In anguish*) Do not leave me altogether *alone*!
. . . Well! As it turns out, I am not horrified. So. I can
go through easily, with my hands. And reaching out—all
my arms. There are other persons here, somebody to talk
to, a present company. Turn on the lights. (*The houselights go on*) Dear audience—you are the audience—allow
me.

*(At this point the woman, no longer "*FAUSTINA,*" will speak or behave however she happens to on the occasion. At one performance the actress fell into a panic of stage-fright and fled. That too was very well. But it will be just as it is, however it is)*

Curtain

Comment on *Faustina*

This legend of the court of Marcus Aurelius is mentioned in Kurt Seligmann's *Mirror of Magic*. The outcome of the experiment as I describe it is not legendary, but it is psychologically more likely. With someone as strong-minded and lusty as Faustina, the shock of the experience would not result in frigidity, as planned, but in a further breakthrough. At face value, the ritual is a Mithraic *taurobolium*; but the same ambiguity persists. Is the purpose of such a rite to bolster the order of the State by freezing excitement into it, or is it to renew society by releasing an animal spirit?

I have tried to incorporate the physical space of the stage into the fable. The setting of the first scene is the body of the dreamer stretched out in sleep; the action is his wish. The closed setting of the second scene is inside his head, a displacement upward as anxiety increases. Breaking through the proscenium at the end vividly means to me breaking through into life, out of art.

For the life of art as I have practiced it for twenty years is not very endurable: to increase the tensions of insight and feeling to a climax of—words. My teeth ache with it. It has occurred to me to give up writing, but why should I spitefully disown my powers? No, what is wrong is repeating the unsatisfactory ending; the image ought to make itself real. That is, the play must get me into physical contact with the audience. Freud said it succinctly: frustrated in love and luck and esteem, an artist retires into his dream and shapes this in an art-work and thereby wins love, fortune and fame. But I am impatient, and that which must come about indirectly—the audience coming to me because of what I am—I try to realize directly, reaching through to the audience.

Nevertheless, I am not *merely* making a mistake. I am dreaming a different kind of dream, of social institutions more amenable than our civilization with its theatre of frozen spectators. It has been the longing now of three generations of playwrights to create a theatre of participation. They have changed the architecture, the setting, the direction, to bring the play into the audience. But the result is still not achieved. The words are still the artist's, even though they might be spoken out front. Obviously we can speak only our own words, we cannot respond *for* the audience. We lay baits and wire shocks—in the epilogue to this play I try simple cajolery—asking the audience to take the hint and rise and move in a circle. And tear the artist limb from limb?—no more artist!—and tear down the theatre and the State.

In the character of Marcus Aurelius, I try to analyze a system of philosophic ideas as a specific character-defense with its accompanying affects (and affectlessness). The long speeches are culled from *The Golden Book*. And what I have tried to portray in the second scene is the desperate search for the right use of speech altogether. The problem poses itself as follows: Why should a protagonist in tragic extremity waste his time and breath in talking, just because this is a theatrical convenience? It seems to me that all the tragedies are unrealistic in this point. So my gladiator can cry only "Help! help!" But this, continued, would not be very interesting on the stage, though it is profoundly interesting in the world.

Or the question poses itself: Why am I writing these fairly syntactical sentences rather than clamping my teeth and keeping from crying, "Help! help!"?

Both the gladiator and myself come to a thought that allows us to speak again: namely, that under certain circumstances it is *pleasant* to use words and feel the flow of reasons. And even Marcus has a reason to speak (that I share with him):

MARCUS   Why does he harp on this one word? Is that the spontaneous outcry in such a case?

FRONTO   What would you cry out in such a case?

MARCUS   I am in such a case, and I am crying out.

Jonah

Characters

JONAH	GUIDE
ANGEL	DANCERS
WIFE	FIRST SPY
CHILD	SECOND SPY
CAPTAIN	CROWD
IDOLATORS	SOLDIER
VARIOUS SAILORS	SINGER
SEASICK PASSENGER	GIRL
MEDITATIVE MAN	COURTIER
VARIOUS PASSENGERS	DUCHESS
TAILOR	DUKE
BAILIFF	KING
LITTLE PATIENT	LADY
DOCTOR	ASTROLOGER
NURSE	VARIOUS NINEVITES
SECOND DOCTOR	MESSENGER
PEASANT	WORM

N. B. Assign the actors double or triple similar roles as much as possible, to create the effect of a few character-types and JONAH.

ACT ONE

JONAH's home: a poor room wth a door and a window in the rear wall. A bed on the left in which the prophet's wife is asleep; an inner door in the right wall. JONAH is a fat little Jew, in a nightshirt. He tiptoes in from the room on the right, turns back the cover, kisses his sleeping wife.

JONAH Now I lay me down to sleep—it's all right, I won't get to sleep. In ten minutes, just when one eye is closing after the other, the little one begins to bawl. Next, the moment after I have dropped off, comes the Lord of Hosts, crying, "Sleeper, awake! Awake! Rise! Go!" So I *won't* get my sleep . . . Luckily I have the knack of dozing when people are talking to me. This gives me my reputation for being firm . . . Now I lay me down to sleep, I pray the Lord my soul to keep.

> *(He blows out the lamp. The room is moonlit. As soon as his head hits the pillow, he begins to snore. The baby in the next room cries for an instant, but JONAH continues sleeping. An ANGEL, somewhat radiant, pokes his head in at the window.)*

ANGEL Look at him! Dreaming away the delights of his first to his fourth years. Well, that's enough romance.
> *(Three thunderous knocks at the door. JONAH turns over. One more knock.)*

JONAH Mama! . . . *(Like a baby)* Waah-wa! The baby's crying, get up. *(He pushes his wife)* Gewalt! He's here again. *(There is a thunderous blow at the door)* I'm always awaking when there is a loose connection between the body and the soul. No wonder I have a short temper.

Sweetheart! Let me catch hold of the tail end of my little dream. (*He falls back like a stone. But there's a loud knock. He sits up*) It should happen to a dog to be a prophet of the Lord of Hosts . . . Maybe—who knows— it's a mistake and He wants to go next door.

VOICE OF ANGEL   Jonah!

JONAH   No mistake. The Lord of Hosts, of *Hosts*, and me he picks on. (*He peeks out the window*) It is the Lord of Hosts. Two o'clock by Orion in midsummer. I've gotten to know the stars of the unusual hours.

VOICE OF ANGEL   *Jonah!*

JONAH   Burst a blood vessel! . . . Why should I commit myself? Why should I commit myself to the extent of opening the door? Suppose I really had some business of my own to attend to? (*Calls*) Congress is in session; come back in half an hour. (*Cackles*)

VOICD OF ANGEL   JONAH! (*The house quakes*) Don't go back to sleep, you know the nightmare you have.
    (*Wildly* JONAH *throws open the door, disclosing the* ANGEL)

ANGEL   (*Sharply*)   Always I must call three times!

JONAH   (*Enraged*)   You! Get out of my house! . . . One, two, three—out! (*He shoves the* ANGEL *out and slams the door on his own finger*) Owww! (*There is tussling at the door. Desperately* JONAH *begins to pile up a barricade of furniture. His* WIFE *awakes*)

WIFE (*Sleepily*)   What's now?

JONAH Now she's asking what's! She's sleeping while I slam my finger in the door. Owww!

WIFE What *are* you doing in the middle of the night?

JONAH He's here again. So you'll help me push the bureau, I shouldn't get a rupture—

WIFE If you're going away again, honey, please this time leave me some money in the pot. (*They push the furniture. The baby begins to cry. The* ANGEL *steps lightly through the window*) You woke the baby up, you dope. Why do you have to make so much noise for?

JONAH Ha!
  (*He leaps at the* ANGEL *and they wrestle. The* WIFE *hits the* ANGEL *with a pan*)

WIFE Blessed be he who comes in the name of the Lord. (*The* ANGEL *lightly tosses* JONAH *across the room, where he sits, stunned*)

ANGEL Who do you think you are, father Jacob?

WIFE Gorilla!
  (*The* ANGEL *lights the lamp. The child is crying loudly*)

ANGEL Madam, your child is crying.
  (*He touches the wall, which starts to fall; he summons it to stand again, which it does*)

WIFE *Nebich!* A regular Samson. So you'll leave my house intact. Maybe you have some other feats of strength to show me after I've had a cup of coffee. (*Calls*) It's all right, little mousey, Mama is coming. Only when he goes

135

away this time, you should tell him to leave me some money in the pot.

(Exit into the other room, slamming the door. JONAH *meanwhile is rolling his head and sucking on his thumb)*

ANGEL   Man, arise! Arise, I said.

JONAH   I'm sitting here dying and he's asking me to do calisthenics.

ANGEL   *(Inexorably)*   Go to Nineveh, that great city, and cry out against it.

*(*JONAH *has leapt to his feet)*

JONAH   No! . . . Ow. *(He bends over in pain)*

ANGEL   Say, "Yet forty days and Nineveh shall be destroyed!"

JONAH   To Nineveh? There I'll be popular! A prophet they need, you should pardon the expression, like a pain in the arm. No!

ANGEL   No?

JONAH   No! No!

ANGEL   What do you mean no?

JONAH   What do you mean what do I mean? I mean drop dead!

ANGEL   I beg your pardon—

JONAH   It's all right, I'm not offended. *(Abashed)* My Lord —look at the matter, just once, the way I see it. You say, "Arise! go to Nineveh!" So I arise and I go to Nineveh. "Cry out that Nineveh will be destroyed." So I *cry* out that Nineveh will be destroyed. So then Nineveh *is* destroyed. Then! Then everybody who walks along the street looks at me out of the corner of his eyes and mutters, "Here comes Jonah! What a Jonah!" So what can I say? I say drop dead! Or contrariwise: I cry out that Nineveh will be destroyed, and suppose Nineveh is *not* destroyed—who can tell? Then everybody who comes along laughs himself sick! What can I say then? I say—drop dead! So right here and now, before I start out and make a spectacle of myself, I might as well say drop dead! (*He cackles away at his joke*) You see, it's a joke—I didn't mean you personally . . . Owww.

(*A moment's pause—and the tears begin to roll down* JONAH's *face*)

ANGEL (*Gently*)   What's the matter, old man?

JONAH (*Passionately, near sobbing*)   What's the matter?! This is the question that the Angel asks the prophet of the Lord of Hosts! *What's the matter?* (*More lightly*) The matter he's asking what's! I'm sixty-five years old and my only well-wisher is the undertaker. What's the matter! I walk in the street and B. says to A., "You think you got *tsures*? Wait! Here comes Jonah." I show up at a wedding and the bride has a miscarriage. What's the matter. (*Bitterly*) The matter, my Lord, the matter—did you once give me some *good* news to cry out? Not *me*, especially, why should *I* be honored? but *was* there once some good news? . . . I'm not thinking of anything splendid, but just for once an encouraging word—for instance, that the war *won't* break out, or that a politician will do a sensible thing, or maybe that Jessie will have twins and there won't be a plague.

ANGEL Man, do you do well to be so angry?

JONAH I'm not thinking even of a change for the better; simply, "Man, arise! Cry out that next year won't be any worse!"

ANGEL Do you have to be a prophet to predict that everything will go from bad to worse? This is an historical law of His glorious order.

JONAH (*Bursts into tears*) Nebich!

ANGEL (*After a pause, whispering*) There will one day be good news.
    (*He whispers in* JONAH's *ear. They talk unintelligible words*)

JONAH (*Passionately*) When? If not now, when?

ANGEL All in good time.

JONAH Meantime!—

ANGEL Meantime you must do everything in turn—whatever comes to your hand.

JONAH Small comfort—

ANGEL Nay, but some—

JONAH —is to be got from knowing that whatever I turn my hand to is a necessary evil. I'd rather not commit myself at all.

ANGEL This you cannot do.

JONAH Oh yes! Because I have no confidence that what I say will come to good—because I know, in fact, that the reverse is true—I have perfected a thousand ways of keeping quiet. I can show that many more things have to be taken into consideration. When I am hard pressed—because people really need to *know*—I often lapse into silent sympathy . . . At least, when I don't commit myself to it, they can't say that the inevitable calamity has been my doing. If only I could inwardly remain in doubt; but then *you* come and compel me to speak out against my better judgment.

ANGEL Jonah, suppose that just because you warned them, the catastrophe would one time be averted.

JONAH Thank you; now I should be a liar. Not bad enough to prophesy disaster, I must prophesy falsely, when really some quite different disaster is going to take place! . . . Praise be to the Lord of Hosts, when I cry out that a local disaster is about to take place, at least it never fails to take place. And when I don't cry out, it also takes place.

ANGEL Jonah, rejoice! You will be famous in history. You are the first of the prophets who will foretell disaster not only to the Jews but also to the Gentiles.

JONAH *How* have the Gentiles managed up till now!

ANGEL (*Sternly*) Right! Up to now they were swept away like dust when the wind howls. Now each one *knows* that he is doomed for his sins.

JONAH Oh? Is this an advantage?

ANGEL Of course. You'd be surprised how much satisfaction these people get in feeling guilty. And how much resentment they can exhaust against the prophet who has foretold them the news.

JONAH Namely me.

ANGEL How many fewer curses assail Him when people take a little cognizance of the morrow and think a little who and what they are? What one is, no, Jonah?

JONAH (*Humbly*) It's true. All flesh is as the grass. (*Bows*)

ANGEL (*Touches him ritually and raises him. Aside*) I can't help it. I love this old mixture of humility and a little absolute skepticism. He is armed against the very worst that I could wish him.

JONAH (*Dryly*) Glory to God in the Highest—such as it is!

ANGEL Amen.

WIFE (*Looking into the room*) I made some coffee.
(*She exits*)

JONAH Good. Will you have some coffee with us?

ANGEL If it's no trouble.
(*She brings in two cups and sugar, and returns again with a cup for herself and carrying the* CHILD *on her arm*)

JONAH See the little mouse! . . . Sugar?

ANGEL It's a little girl. Eighteen months? See the mother and the little girl and a cup of coffee, standing in the doorway . . . (*To* JONAH) Please.

WIFE This is Suzannah. See the company? Say hello to the company, Susie.
(*The* CHILD *merely stares*)

ANGEL You two are lucky to have a child at your ages.
(JONAH *gives the* CHILD *a lump of sugar, which she solemnly nibbles*)

WIFE   She's company when I'm left here alone. The others are grown up and gone.

JONAH   She don't seem to have much to say tonight.

WIFE   She's not used to being up at night, to see what it's like at night. Naturally she can only look and look.

ANGEL   (*In the manner of Rilke*)   I have seen that look— that looks outside, only outside.

WIFE   Say good-bye to the company, Susie.
(*Exeunt, the* CHILD *staring over her shoulder*)

CHILD'S VOICE   (*Piercing*)   Goo-byyy! Goo-byyyyyy!

JONAH   I watch her and every day I come to remember something important about myself. I hate to go away for a single day for fear I'll miss the important thing that I can't remember. It wasn't so with the others. At that time I still used to imagine that I had a life of my own to lead.

ANGEL   (*Sipping coffee*)   Even if you hurry, the journey to Nineveh will take eight days. Now go to sleep and start early in the morning. Here are the tickets . . . Let me tell you something about that great city. The men of Nineveh have been to school to the extremes—they have had it— they are doctors of the Last Resort. There is no use in appealing to them by prudential considerations, by saying that such and such will lead to certain advantages, because they think they have already experienced all those advantages. Just tell them that the jig's up; this will make a profound impression. The fact is that, unlike your Jews, the Ninevites are honest enough to admit the relation between their private vices and their public benefits. They have a foolish standard of living and it keeps the economy

141

going. You may learn something from them. They are
quite without illusions—except as a whole. The king is
even a kind of philosopher—wait till you meet him! You'll
see what I mean. You'll be amazed what all this comes
to. They're like little girls and boys. Just at the moment,
they are mighty imperialists; they have conquered everything and they rule over everything. From our point of
view, this has resulted in their collecting hundreds of new
idols, one from every town. But they don't believe in *any*
of them any more.

JONAH O.K., you've sold me. What shall I say to them?

ANGEL I told you. Say, "Yet forty days and Nineveh shall
be destroyed!" and then sit it out. This requires no explanation. They will themselves provide plenty of ex-
planations. I leave the rest to your own judgment. Here,
for Suzannah. (*He produces a huge pink Easter rabbit out
of his hat*) Good-bye, dear old man.
         (*Exit.* JONAH *looks after him out the window*)

JONAH Gone! . . . For God's sake, look at the house. All
for nothing. (*Setting things to rights*) One thing at least
is sure—I got a broken thumb . . . The nail is turning
black. Hephzibah! . . .

VOICE OF WIFE Shhh.

JONAH Here he snuk in like a burglar. There he walks out
like a gentleman, after pushing the sofa out of the way.
Here he tossed me up—and here I sat. (*In a stage
whisper*) Zibah! . . . (*Pause*) If I *believed* in the destruc-
tion of Nineveh, that great city, wouldn't I hurry to the
ends of the earth—and in the right direction—to cry it
out? But where is any difference between that Nineveh

yesterday and tomorrow? They've been going at it at the same clip for years—I know the whole story; does he think I lived in Gath-Hepher all my life, just because I talk with a provincial accent? Take it from me, prophecy won't do any good. The fact is that such threats, especially when they turn out fatally, are just what they thrive on. I'm a plain man, and to tell the truth, I never make a prediction unless I see a use for it. Some allowance has to be made for unexpected bad luck. This is not so absurd, it happened to me once. A bolt from the blue—and goodbye to all that. It's only afterwards that you see it was inevitable. Take—why did the Tower of Babel collapse just when it was 35,412 feet high? A fault in the engineering, of course. But at the time, it looked awful.

WIFE He's gone?

JONAH Gone but not forgotten. Listen, you'll help me pack my little satchel. I've got to get out of here quick. (*Business*)

WIFE Just like this, in the middle of the night? Where are you going this time?

JONAH Put in the salts, I'll have to take a ship.

WIFE A ship? And where are you going in a ship?
(*The* ANGEL *looks in at the window—unnoticed*)

JONAH I'll catch a boat at Joppa, and I'm off to Tarshish.

WIFE Tarshish! After all these years he's sending you back to the small towns!

JONAH Why shouldn't I visit Isaac and see what his boys are like?

WIFE   What! an Angel wakes you up in the middle of the night to tell you to visit Isaac who is coming here next month for the holidays?

JONAH   Maybe.

WIFE   You liar!

JONAH   (*Angry*)   *His* idea is I should go to Nineveh, that great city; *my* idea is I should get in hell out o' here and go to Tarshish. Nineveh (*Points with his thumb*) is that way; Tarshish (*Points with his other thumb*) is this way.

WIFE   Jonah! Why on earth do you want to do such a thing?

JONAH   Do you think I know? This I've got to find out.

WIFE   (*Sitting down*)   Do what you want. Only afterwards, don't blame me.

JONAH   (*Cheerfully*)   Maybe I never told you about the uses of the five fingers? So watch! . . . The first finger is the finger pointing out directions. Thus, upstate? (*With his thumb*) this way. Downtown? That way. The second finger is the pointing down finger. Thus (*Pointing down with his index finger*), this piece of goods, I should let it go for twelve ninety-five, a penny less I'm losing money . . . The middle finger is for political discussions (*A horizontal sweep*)—Pharaoh? He hasn't got a chance! . . . The fourth finger is the esthetic finger. The Queen of Sheba? (*A dainty circle of the thumb and fourth finger*) Ah, a beauty! . . . And the pinkie finger (*Picking his nose with it*)—I can't remember what the pinkie finger is for.

  (*The* ANGEL *laughs heartily in the window, and vanishes*)

WIFE *Nu?*

JONAH So nothing! Good-bye, good riddance! . . . (*He seizes the satchel*) Good-bye, dear.

WIFE Jonah! Leave me money in the pot.

JONAH How much is there?
(*She takes down the pot and there is a large roll of bills.* JONAH *devoutly*) Thanks be to God who gives us our daily bread.

JONAH (*Devoutly*) Thanks be to God who gives us our daily bread. How much does it come to?

WIFE (*Counting*) Sixty—eighty—one hundred—one hundred forty, one, two, three—one hundred and forty-four dollars.

JONAH I'll be gone for eight weeks. He's now paying eighteen dollars a week and expenses.
(*A kiss. Exit* JONAH. *She sees the rabbit and cries after him out the window*)

WIFE Hey! What's this?

Curtain

ACT TWO

(*To be played rapidly. A rocking ship at sea—a tilting cartoon front that the actors play behind. Wind howling. The passengers are propitiating their gods. One is pissing, another is in profound meditation. One is shouting "Loolooloo," another, "Elelel."* JONAH *is asleep in a conspicuously inconspicuous place.*)

VOICES ALOFT Laaaar! Coming around.

ANOTHER VOICE Look out!
(*The boom swings over and the boat is now rocking on the other side. Loud crash*)

CAPTAIN Son of a bitch, *jibing* you mean. Haul 'em close. (*Aside*) Hell of a lot of good it'll do.

FIRST IDOLATOR Loolooloo, Loolooloo . . .

CAPTAIN As much good in Lulu as in what I'm doing, and that's a fact . . . All the way down! . . . Hey, sailor, what in hell are these people doing?

A SAILOR Each one is praying to his own god.

IDOLATORS (*Competitively*)
Loolooloo . . .
Elelelel . . .
(*One drowning out the other in triumph*)
Elelel—we win! We win!

CAPTAIN Pray on, prayers! . . . Close! Drop the mizzen. (*He stumbles on a satchel in the gangway*) Frig! Who the frig left this piss-damn suitcase here . . . Hey, all the way down. Down! Up! Up! . . . What are you pissin' about? Pray on, prayers. There's a devil up there who changes the wind. (*He stumbles on a suitcase. He steps on* JONAH. *Beside himself*) What's this lunk sleeping here, when my ship *The Glory of Tammuz* is not long for this world? Too late! Duck!

> (*The boom comes about*)

VOICE ALOFT   Coming arooouund!

SAILORS
> Elelelelel . . .
> Em Em Em Em . . .
> El Em En O Pee!

A SAILOR   This is the passenger who boarded at Joppa, and he's dreaming he's going to Tarshish.

CAPTAIN (*Kicks* JONAH)   Wake up, lunk!

JONAH   Papa!

CAPTAIN   Wake up, passenger who came on at Joppa! Wake up, dreamer of going to Tarshish. You'll never come any nearer to Tarshish than a friggin' hole right down to the sandy bottom. (*Kicks him again*) Can't you see that the others are praying to their piss-dam divinities? Who in hell do you think you are, snorting away in the lap of luxury?

JONAH   Hm. Anti-Semitic.
> (*Noise. Crash. Call of "Coming around." The* CAP-TAIN *leaps at a flying rope.*)

CAPTAIN   Here, make yourself useful. Grab hold o' this here sheet—this one here—and hang on, hang on—close!
> (JONAH *hangs on. A wash of water comes over the side*)

JONAH (*Drenched*) *Weh's mir.* What goes on here? I was dreaming of bouncing on my Mama. And she was singing me a little song. Da dee dum dee, dee doo dahhh—

(*The* CAPTAIN *stumbles over the satchel*)

CAPTAIN In the name o' the Mother and the Son, what goddamn lunk left this piss-damn satchel in the fuckin' gangway?

JONAH Dee dee doo da dee doo dum . . . tsk, such language.

CAPTAIN Will y' get this friggin satchel outta my way before I toss it over?

JONAH Dee dee dum! Dee dee doo!

CAPTAIN O.K.! You asked for it!
(*He tosses over the satchel*)

JONAH (*Singing*) Dee dee doo, it ain't my satchel! Da dee dee . . . Ugh. (*He staggers to the rail, seasick. Business of storm increases.* JONAH *says apologetically*) I always get sick when I sing the old songs at myself (SAILORS *rush by*) Where are they running? Sailor! Which way am I supposed to run? (*To* SEASICK PASSENGER) Do you know what's up?

SEASICK PASSENGER I'm afraid I'll die and I'm afraid I won't.
(*A spar falls*)

JONAH *Gewalt!*

VOICE ALOFT Yaaaaaaar!

CAPTAIN What's *he* want?

SAILOR ON BRIDGE What in hell do *you* want? (*Faint call from above*) He says that something's peculiar!

CAPTAIN He's bang right, my ship is sinking.

JONAH (*Calling aloft*) He says you're bang right, the friggin ship is sinking.

SAILOR ON BRIDGE He says come up and see for yourself.

JONAH Who, me? (*He rushes to the ladder; the* CAPTAIN *pushes him out of the way*) This is amazing! Is it always like this? I've never been to sea before. You know I got on at Joppa and now I'm in the thick of everything. Did you see the way I handled the ropes? What do you think friggin means? (*A spar falls next to him*) For heaven's sake, a man could be killed here!

CAPTAIN (*In towering excitement*) He's right. There's no storm anywhere on the high sea. When you look from the crow's nest, the sun is shining clear (*Shock, the ship heels over*)—the sea is becalmed—it's a pleasure to see. Come up, all of you, and have a look.
(*Five spars fall*)

SAILOR *The Glory of Tammuz* is bewitched!

MEDITATIVE MAN Like the thoughts of an angry man—

JONAH Ha! I know him!

MEDITATIVE MAN To him, everything looks black—

JONAH True!

MEDITATIVE MAN But outside his narrow vision, the universe is quiet. This *rage* is moving through the calm sea.
(*Pause*)

JONAH

JONAH   Captain, cast lots and find out who it is in the belly of the ship who is warping the winds and stirring the whirlpool up.

CAPTAIN   Frig! I thought we needed seamanship and navigation, to sink us according to the most advanced techniques. It turns out to be a case for mental concentration and guessing the will of a malicious devil. (*He burrs his lips with his finger, to mean "Crazy."*)

> (*The* SAILORS *have gathered round in a circle. The rocking of the ship ceases*)

A SAILOR   A devil!
> (*The light dims*)

ANOTHER SAILOR   It's getting dark.

ANOTHER SAILOR   A whirlpool is opening in the water.

A PASSENGER   It seems to be letting up.

MEDITATIVE MAN   No, it's gathering power. The next blow will be the last.

SEVERAL   Let us pray.
> (*They kneel. The* CAPTAIN *passes around a bucket and each chooses a lot in silence*)

JONAH (*Holding up the black lot*)   See, it's me.

CAPTAIN   Who are you, little man? Tell us, why is this evil come upon us? Where are you from? Of what people are you? What is your business on my ship?

JONAH (*In the center. Twilight*)   I am a Hebrew, and I fear Jehovah, the creator of the sea and sky.

CAPTAIN   I remember you. Why did you not pray to *your* god, when everybody else was praying to his?

JONAH   Because Jehovah said to me, "Man, arise! go to Nineveh that great city and cry out against it!"—I came aboard at Joppa instead.

CAPTAIN   Why did you?

JONAH   I hoped to run away at least to Tarshish. But He has found me out in the middle of the sea . . . Listen, there is going to be a thunderclap.
    (*There is a light thunderclap*)

SEVERAL   Woe!

JONAH   (*Passionately*)   Let me die now and not cause any more trouble. When I look and see how I am forced always to choose the lesser of two evils, but never any good that I have faith in—I refuse any longer to commit myself to it. Yes, I too know that when I don't commit myself, I have committed myself to the evils that exist. And when I'm dead, so far as I'm concerned they'll be forever. Nevertheless!

MEDITATIVE MAN   Old man, you're a coward. The thing is to have another ounce of strength.

JONAH   You're right; but I don't.

CAPTAIN   Have a heart, don't upbraid him with moral arguments when you see he is on the way to despair . . . Old man, if this is how it is with you, you have an angry mind and no place where you move will be quiet.

JONAH   *You*'re right. When I think of who and where I am, I feel the terrible abyss of a storm that is about to burst . . . Say! (*Entire change of mood*) Do you know the joke about the Rabbi who says, "You're right?"

SAILOR (*Indignant*) A joke? Is this the time for jokes? When our ship is about to sink, he has time for jokes?

JONAH (*To the sailor*) You're right. You're right.

CAPTAIN (*To* JONAH) No, *you're* right! *Rely* upon the bright side, it will give you courage. You know, as a sea captain I often have to give advice to people entrusted to my care; and there is nothing so helpful, I have found, as to concentrate on some bright little item. So tell us the joke.

JONAH Oh, we Jews have a special kind of jokes. They consist in happy little anecdotes founded on absolute despair. There is nothing so consoling as to realize that everything is worse than you could possibly imagine. After all, it can't be so bad as all that! And then you shrug your shoulders and say *Nebich*.

CAPTAIN *Nebich?* What is this *Nebich?* Is he a fetish?

JONAH It means—it means that this big deal that you have is as *nothing* compared with a little secret that *I* know; so really there is no need for me to feel the burning resentment that I do feel; and anyway, I have my own ideas about the value of that little secret, such as it is. *Nebich!* . . . Yes, he is a fetish! (*Passionately*) Captain! Take this nebichist and for the good of all cast him into the sea! So will the sea become calm to you, because it is on my account that there is this great storm.

SAILORS Yes! Throw him overboard.

SAILOR He says there is a devil whose name is Nebich.
(*They rush at him*)

CAPTAIN (*Protecting him*) You sons o' bitches, lay your friggin hands off! The first one that touches this old man goes head first in the soup himself. He paid his fare at Joppa and he's my passenger. Do I hear anybody say no?
(*They fall back. There is a rumble of thunder*)

CAPTAIN Brave boys. You're willing to toss an old man to the fishes in order to save your lousy skins. We'll take our chances.
(*The ship lists*)

JONAH Let them do as I say.

CAPTAIN Back to your oars! Shut up, Nebich, I'm in charge of this ship. *The Glory of Tammuz* is enlisted on the side of this passenger against the devil, whoever he is, and we'll ride into Tarshish on strokes of oars.
(*Lightning. A violent shock. The sailors go to their posts*)

VOICE ALOFT Coming around and around and around.

CAPTAIN I have come to love this little old man like my dead father.
(*Wash from all directions*)

JONAH It's no use, sailors . . . I never wept until I saw the courage of these willing sailors; but now I can't help crying. (*Weeps*) I'm glad I've seen a human act, a vain one, the last thing before I die.

A SAILOR (*Running in*) The oars are broke.

CAPTAIN Take up the man and throw him into the sea.
(*The* SAILORS *raise* JONAH *up*)

JONAH Wait! Captain! Is that my little satchel?

153

CAPTAIN (*Tragically*) Sure is your little satchel.
　　(*He gives it to* JONAH)

A SAILOR　Hebrew, tell your God that we are not responsible for this evil deed.

ANOTHER SAILOR　Let us not perish for this man's life. Lay not innocent blood upon us.

CAPTAIN　I tried as long as possible to keep this prophet with us.

SAILORS　Heave!

JONAH　Hear, O Israel, the Lord our God, the Lord is One.
　　(*There is a flash as they heave* JONAH *over the side. The Fish's nose appears an instant. A great shout from all, crowding to the rail*)

ALL

　　Leviathan!
　　Did *you* see it?
　　Did you see what I saw?
　　The Sea Monster.

A SAILOR　A big fish rose out of the water and swallowed him up when we tossed him over. Everybody saw it, not only me!
　　(*With comic rapidity the ship ceases to rock. The scene brightens. The fallen spars leap aloft to return to the masts. Other things rearrange themselves*)

VOICES　The oars are whole. The sails are up.

MEDITATIVE MAN　Wait! Maybe the hopes I lost years ago will revive.

PASSENGER   Nothing is gone except the old man and one little satchel.

ANOTHER PASSENGER *(Tragically)*   *My* satchel's gone too.
   (His satchel comes flying over the rail)

CAPTAIN   No, here it comes, good as new. I see I was wrong to be so stubborn about keeping the prophet. The sea is full of sails—and the sky is full of birds.

VOICE ALOFT   Land ho!

SAILORS   Land ho! Land ho!

CAPTAIN   It's amazing. Now I find it hard even to remember the Hebrew.

MEDITATIVE MAN   Let us offer a sacrifice.
   (A pigeon is brought, which the CAPTAIN *offers, cutting its throat, while the others stand around)*

CAPTAIN   This Jonah—for the name Jonah means a Pigeon —we offer Thee in place of the one who escaped.
   (He casts it into the sea)

Curtain

ACT THREE

*To be played slowly and with pauses. Inside the Fish.
Total dark.* JONAH *is heard snoring and wheezing.*

VOICE OF JONAH   Hello? Still dark? I'll try to sleep . . . I
can't sleep; I'm all slept out. I guess this time I slept
around the clock . . . What a feeling! I'm simply washed
out and hung up to dry. Not a dream I haven't dreamed
through!—except this one . . . Say, what's this? Are my
eyes open or closed? This is thick! Hey! Where in hell
am I? Hey! (*He screams*) Hello! . . . Hey! . . . Helloooo!
. . . In the name of the Father and Son, *in the Fish!* I
remember it all! . . . Hey! . . . Maybe I'd better not shout
and move around, it might get her mad . . . I *swam*—the
foam—the teeth, yes! There was a word! (*A loud swash-
ing*) *Gewalt!* Quiet down, you big Fish! . . . Ai, Aiiiiii!
(*Pause. He whispers*) *Nebich.* (*Pause*) Clearly—I mean
darkly—*clearly,* do you hear? (*Shouts*) *Clearly*—I've been
in here more than a single day. It's my second day in
hell. They say it lasts three days . . . The first day I was
dead, period. The second day I begin to look around.
(*A long pause. Then, quietly*)

A man was fighting a losing fight.
"Give this part up," I told him, "turn somewhere
   else and strike."
He did. There was a muffled cry.

"Now fight! here's the place, now's the time."
"I'd rather not," he said.
"Seize the advantage! You've got them by surprise."
"No, here I sit!"

"What was that muffled outcry that you heard?"

"It spoke a word, and *Death* was that one word."

(*A pause. Vigorously*)

Well, I'll see what it's like here, anyway. Very well to sleep—but what when you *can't* sleep. (*Earnestly*) Jonah! A man ought to be able to sleep always, hardly trying; it's the *other*, trying to keep awake, that needs the effort . . . Surely if a man *could* sleep, he could sleep *here*, in this warm, wet, soft and swaying interior. If a man could choose, if he could choose, would he not choose to be *here*. I won't get sick here. (*He starts to hum*) Da dee da di . . . I think I'll experiment. Methodically. Supposing, for instance, I kick her *here*? She rolls! And *there*? . . . Roll away, monster! Dee dee doo da . . . This is great, a regular submarine! Whoaa! Whoa up, monster! . . . And here? Hey! Nix! *Hey!* . . . So sensitive, monster? Have I hurt your feelings? . . . Ai! . . . Da dee da dee dee, di dee da . . . (*He sings*)

Tired is the trouble? I'll carry you an inch!

I'll carry you an inch!

I'll carry you an inch!

Not more than an inch, though!

Not more than an inch, though!

What's that?

(*On one side of the stage a dim scene opens; it is a room with a shade drawn down.* JONAH *as a little* TAILOR *is sitting cross-legged, sewing. The persons are less than adult size and somewhat doll-like in make-up and movement*)

TAILOR (*Singing*) *Ut azoi*, sings the Tailor!

(*Enter an angelic Beau Brummell; he is the* ANGEL *of Act One, dollified and dandified*)

ANGEL   Tailor! I want you should be making me a pair of trousers! There's a party in heaven—don't ask—a wedding. At the full moon, on the fifteenth of Heshvan. Why should I exaggerate—God will be there! . . . There should be, for God's sake, no cuffs; but over the pockets maybe little pleats, no? The latest style.

TAILOR   So calm yourself . . . First we take the measurement. The pants *you*'ll wear, the cut is up to me You go, I lie down, and it comes to me in a dream!
(*Exit* ANGEL; *the* TAILOR *lies down. Re-enter* ANGEL)

ANGEL   Tailor! My pair of trousers!

TAILOR   Not yet!

ANGEL   Not yet? What do you mean not yet? The wedding, it takes place at the full moon and my trousers he says not yet! For thirteen days he's dreaming, and what am I supposed to wear?

TAILOR   Listen. If you want you should cover your shapely legs with a pair of leggings like a farmer, so you don't need to come to Jonah the Tailor, in business, I wouldn't say much, for sixty-five years. If it's a pair of *trousers* you want, then generally I lie down and it comes to me in a dream.
(*Exit* ANGEL, *etc. Re-enter* ANGEL)

ANGEL   Tailor! Do you have my pair of trousers? The wedding is tomorrow.

TAILOR   Yes. Last night I had a dream—and in this dream— I saw a pair of pants. *Here* are the pants. So you'll try them on, please.
(*Mimicry with mimic mirror, etc.*)

ANGEL   Beautiful! My breath—is taken away. Should I say they're not beauties? . . . But for God's sake, Tailor! such a long time! In six days the Lord God made the whole world, and you take two weeks for a pair of pants!

TAILOR   My good fellow—come, here let me show you something. (*He pulls up the shade*) Ordinarily I don't look out of this window . . . My good fellow—so you'll *look* at the world, and you'll look at this pair of pants.
(*Blackout. At once another scene is illuminated nearer to him, about midstage.* DOCTORS, *a* NURSE, *all huge in comparison with the* PATIENT, *a little* JONAH *of less than five*)

BAILIFF   Next case! Bring out the little bastard!

LITTLE PATIENT   (*Roughly pushed*)   Don't shove! You see what my father got for shoving.

BAILIFF   What?

LITTLE PATIENT   Me, you dope.

DOCTOR   What's the indictment?

LITTLE PATIENT   Look here! I came here for a medical examination; I'm not on *trial* for anything. Nurse! I want you should be looking at my horgan.
(*Business to one side with the* NURSE)

NURSE   Your organ is perfectly all right.

LITTLE PATIENT (*Crowing*)   Yah! Ain't it a beauty!

DOCTOR   We're ready. (*They stretch him out on a table. Auscultation. Consultation*) There's plenty of courage in that little belly, but he seems to be sick at heart.

SECOND DOCTOR   The trouble is that he stays his hand, he stays his hand . . . You may think this is a curious opinion, but I say that if he'd let fly one punch, the oppression in the midriff would disappear.

DOCTOR   This is really a remarkable case; did you ever before see a lad with too much savvy to act out what he himself believes in—because he has a keen suspicion as to what *that's* worth . . . Therefore, he acts on the negative principle of not allowing himself to be pushed.

SECOND DOCTOR   He's been pushed plenty. Look at these bruises.

DOCTOR   Yes, but did he move? Let me tell you—this lad is going to act anyway—

BAILIFF   Gentlemen, gentlemen, have you arrived at a verdict?
> (*They whisper, while the* LITTLE PATIENT *follows the discussion with frightened glances. Blackout*)

VOICE OF JONAH   Aaiiiiiiiiiiiiiiiiii! Auuuuuuuuuuuuuuuuuu! . . . Monster! Monster! Forgive me for causing you the agony that is moment by moment destroying me. Auoo! . . . What blasted fool persuaded me to flee to this hot wet place? (*He shrieks. Exhausted, he whispers*) Nebich . . . I can sleep now. . . . Tomorrow I'll break loose from this living tomb or be dead forever.
> (*Croons*)
> Sleep—sleep—little little little mouse
> *nebich nebich nebich nebich*
> sleep—sleep—little mouse
> (*There is a very long pause, perhaps with music. Then, rhythmic and exalted*)
Forward! Carried forward through the space o' the deep, where even if I were sitting astride the forehead of the

Fish and between his eyes, I should never see a distinguish-
ing landmark to learn where I am or how far I've come
or how far I am still to go—but forward, forward . . . Unless, maybe, it's *backward*! for in such a plight as mine
there's no use in having adventurous ideas! But if you
don't know where you are, what difference does it make
if you go forward or backward? It comes to the same thing.
And maybe she's going around in large circles! These
monsters are generally quite stupid and *they* don't know
where they're going either, so long as there's food; they
pass through the same places again and again. So far as
I'm concerned even this comes to the same thing. Because
it's always *later* . . . The Lord only knows where this monster is heading for, but my life is heading in only one
direction—and this *I* know well. Yet just today—it's *pleasant* in here—gently swaying from side to side . . . She seems
to *like* to swim through these illimitable dark seas, onward
and onward, or round and round . . . I raise up my hand
to feel the passage of time, and I feel it both outside and
inside . . . Surely we are either bound somewhere or it is
a matter of indifference. *At the appointed time—not appointed by me*—but luckily I am not a person to stand on
my dignity—*I shall have arrived*!

(Psalm)

I cried for my troubles unto You, O Lord, and You
  heard me.
Out of the belly of Hell I cried, and You heard my
  voice.

I was thrown in the deep, in the troughs of the seas,
where the waves broke over me, not smoothly.

It was You who cast me there and said *Swim! Swim!*
My hands were tied behind my back: You said *Swim!*
  Swim!

I thought, shall I turn my face to the Lord?
Now is the time that I am out of sight.

The waters closed and I was in the weeds,
  among the hills on the bottom of the sea.

Then my soul fainted. It was turned to You;
  my prayer, such as it is, stands in Your holy place.

And I say, *Salvation comes of the Lord!*
(*Pause. A lamplight near* JONAH, *disclosing him in rags. The lamp is held by the* ANGEL)
  Ah, it's you.

ANGEL Yes, child.

JONAH I am *ashamed* to meet you here, in this condition I am in.

ANGEL Where else should I expect to meet you except in this low place?

JONAH (*Bitterly*) I seem to have a *method* for ending up in this kind of impasse.

ANGEL (*Sharply*) Not only you, Jonah! (JONAH *nods humbly*) No, don't kneel!

JONAH Kneel?

ANGEL I thought you might be about to kneel—and then what would *I* say next?

JONAH My friend, just because I'm in the condition of spending three days in a fish's belly, do you think that I'm completely off my head, to kneel to an appearance? (*In sudden terror*) Ai!

ANGEL What now?

JONAH And what if you also are *just* an appearance—like those dreams—like those jokes—like those dreams. Often a man in my condition begins to have delusions.

ANGEL Child, were those rags of yours in the dreams, and that white hair?

JONAH Why not? If I dreamed what I did, I could dream also about wearing rags and growing old. (*The* ANGEL *touches him*) Blessed art Thou, O Lord, my present salvation.

ANGEL Ah, now you think that salvation comes of the Lord.

JONAH (Sharply) I beg your pardon, I do not think, I *know* salvation is of the Lord—this has not been a matter of *conjecture* with me.

ANGEL (*Sharply*) Why then did you run away?

JONAH I ran, but did I run *away*? This is something new! Is it not said, "If with *all* my heart I *truly* seek him, I shall *surely* find him"? . . . And did He *not* find me?

ANGEL But you say He cast you in before He pulled you out—

JONAH (*Sharply*) Stop right there! When I said so, I did not say so resentfully; it was the simple fact; it was even done with the formality of casting lots.

ANGEL Yes, but did you have to be sarcastic and say He said Swim! Swim!

JONAH (*Angrily*) Well, I *did* swim! And it was He who so advised me. What was wrong in that? I heard a voice cry out, and it said *Swim!*

ANGEL It said Swim? It did not say Death?

JONAH No, not Death! The voice said Swim!

ANGEL And you did swim, old man?

JONAH Yes, I did swim. I swam at least a dozen strokes in the boiling foam—when suddenly I saw nothing but the mouth of the Fish!

ANGEL (*In a strained voice*) Jonah—

JONAH Sir?

ANGEL In heaven—I am not speaking only for myself—the existence of Jonah—

JONAH (*Still sharply*) Am *I* magnifying it?

ANGEL —is *not* a matter of indifference.

JONAH (*Abashed, finds nothing to say for a moment*) Ne-bich. What does it mean practically? Do I or *don't* I exert any influence there?

ANGEL Influence? What is influence? Why do you ask that?

JONAH Frankly—there is a sailor, a Gentile, the captain of a ship called *The Glory of Tammuz*. This man *befriended* me where I did not look for help.

ANGEL I understand you . . . He shall always have a favoring wind.

JONAH (*Bowing deeply*)   My Lord.

ANGEL (*In a loud voice and raising the lamp*)   Now, Jonah!
Jonah! It's the appointed time . . . Leave this place; we
have arrived . . . Go into Nineveh, that great city, and
preach against it the preaching I have told you.

JONAH (*In a strained voice*)   Angel, when I think—that I
have only to *speak* and it's so hard for me—what if I had
also to turn my hand and *do* something for a change?

ANGEL   Please! I'm surprised at you—if you imagine for a
moment that people who are called on to *do* something
have been burdened by the Lord with any second
thoughts. But you intellectuals, who try to persuade other
people, you first have to persuade yourselves. You'd be
shocked if you knew on what level of considerations those
others act, administer justice, wage war. But for stubborn
people like you even the old wars, from long ago, are not
yet over.

JONAH (*Seriously*)   No, they still don't make sense.

ANGEL   Come, old man, we'll talk about these things another time.

JONAH (*Gently*)   Good-bye, Monster.
        (*Darkness, and a rushing music as the curtain falls*)

ACT FOUR

Scene One

A public square in Nineveh. Lively, with pretty continuous music like a county fair. Four or five girls perform an acrobatic ballet, with cartwheels and backflips. Somebody stands on his head while the others look on as at a wonder. A GUIDE *is explaining all this to a* PEASANT.

PEASANT "See Your Empire!" They let us off the land for two weeks' vacation with pay.

GUIDE The idea of this one, old fellow, is that here a person can also stand on his head.

PEASANT Believe me, it was never heard of in the old days.

GUIDE See, she can do it too.

PEASANT You got me! *I* could never do it.

GUIDE Sure you can. You will. Do you think *I* was born within the walls? . . . Why, we have a dog—she'll be along soon—that can walk on two legs and balance a ball on the tip of her nose. She's a beagle.

PEASANT What! That ain't natural.

GUIDE (*Sharply*) Nothing unnatural about it! It's science. We encourage her by feeding her chocolate candy; that's called Reinforcement. We imported the method from Egypt: little by little, easy does it! That's the beauty of Empire.

PEASANT Oh, look here! (*Enter the mask of a cow. The other dancers at once circle her on all fours*) She's good, she is! She's seen a heifer, you bet.

GUIDE Come here. We got this from the country too.
(*They look into the window at the side*)

PEASANT Holy smokes!

GUIDE You see? At bottom—pardon the expression—it's all the same thing. There's nothing new under the sun.

PEASANT I haven't done that since I was twelve years old.
(*Mask of a sheep leans out the window and pats him on the head. Enter* JONAH, *dressed as a dignitary, and shouts in a loud voice*)

JONAH Yet forty days and Nineveh shall be destroyed!
(*There is a roll of thunder. Amazed, the dancers freeze, an arm half lifted, etc. Exit* JONAH, *across the stage*)

PEASANT What's that? Is that part of it?
(*A brief pause*)

DANCERS (*Enthusiastically*)
Crazy! . . .
Did you see the way he wore his hair?
Somebody will make a fortune selling wigs.
Somebody will make a fortune selling thunder.

GUIDE It seems to be a new routine. I never saw it myself.

DANCER (*With great energy*) Yet forty—forty—forty days, and Nineveh shall be destroyed.

DANCERS Woe! Bruuuummm! (*All fall, amazed. Clapping hands*) It's crazy!
(*They go through it again. But there is a shout as two drunken sailors, garlanded, stagger across the stage, and all the* DANCERS, *including the* GUIDE, *throng after*)

them, leaving the PEASANT *behind. Two* SPIES *emerge from the wing and hook him*)

FIRST SPY Stop right there, hayseed, this is a raid! What the hell are you doing away from your field? Talk.

SECOND SPY Where are the guards? Did any of the others escape?

PEASANT (*With pride and dignity*) Hands off, dirt! I am a citizen of Nineveh, and we have no guards any more, since our taxes began to come in from the north. It is the New Imperial Policy, or as we call it, the Nip . . . Don't you know the new laws, you foreigners? You're probably subversives, but—to be perfectly frank with you—I'm too busy to take you in hand. They need me in here—I'm on the Advisory Council—
(*He clambers through the window*)

FIRST SPY There you are, my friend! Just what I told you. Nineveh is a ripe persimmon. One regiment of chariots and they're kaput. It's like taking candy from a baby. Yet forty days and Nineveh will be destroyed—the old booby is bang right. Now (*whispers*)—get going! hip! hip!

SECOND SPY Ain't you coming?

FIRST SPY I said, get going. I have to get some more data.
(*He climbs into the window too. Exit* SECOND SPY)

VOICE OF JONAH Yet forty days and Nineveh shall be destroyed.

CROWD (*Offstage*) Woe! Woe!
(*Shouting, the* CROWD *follows* JONAH *on stage. He looks interestedly into the window. Music sounds within*)

JONAH Hush! Don't talk when there is music playing.

SOLDIER My good fellow! There's always music in Nineveh. Symphonies, song recitals, mixed trios—I can tell you're an out-of-towner; we never listen. But we *could* listen—it's there—it's in the air—it seeps down . . . (*The* SINGER *appears in the window*) No, do listen to this one, she's good.

JONAH Charming! Thanks be to God who has created such a being!

SINGER

> My God, my God, why hast Thou forsaken me
> and at night, and there is no surcease for me.
> I call by day but Thou answerest not,
> and art far from my help at the words of my cry?
> I am a worm and no man,
> a reproach, despised of the people.
> All that see me laugh me to scorn,
> they shoot out the lip, they shake the head:
> "Let him commit himself to the Lord; let Him rescue
> him,
> let *Him* deliver him, seeing He delighteth in him!"
> (*Loud applause*)

JONAH In the name of the Father and the Son, it is a song of King David!

SOLDIER Yes, this mountain music is all the rage now.

GIRL It's a sad song—it makes me feel—oh, it's too much.

SOLDIER Yes, very deep. But note how realistic the observation is. "They shoot out the lip!"—that's good. "They shoot out the lip, they shake the head."

169

GIRL   I'm crazy for the ending, the irony. "Seeing *He* delighteth in him!" I have heard it explained. It seems this David was a boaster, and now he's telling the joke on himself. Whoosh! What a man! It's too much.

JONAH (*Quietly*)   The people here are young, aren't they. I see nothing but boys and girls. Aren't there any old people?

SOLDIER   It's our way of life. So many of us are engaged in youthful activities, we keep our looks for a long time. Then, to tell the truth, we drop off all of a sudden. There just aren't many senior citizens about. But have you seen the King yet? There's a man weighted down with serious cares. To my mind, he's a bit too much of a philosopher.

JONAH   See him? Doesn't he keep himself hidden like other kings?

SOLDIER   Why should he keep himself hidden?

JONAH   Do you think I ought to seek him out and proclaim my prophecy to him?

SOLDIER   Do not fail to do so! He'll be *intensely* interested in what you have to say. (*Suddenly through the window, he sees the* FIRST SPY) Hey! You! Guards!
    (*They rush into the house and pitch the* FIRST SPY, *half dressed, out the window. The* SOLDIER *beats him with a stick*)

SOLDIER (*To* JONAH)   I beg your pardon, stranger. This miserable nonentity imagines he is conspiring against our serene majesty and the security of the city. But the fact is we don't even put the likes of him in the can any more.

(*A kick, and the* FIRST SPY *flies off stage. Laughter. A few stream out of the house and there is a general song and dance*)

ALL

Yet forty forty forty days
and Nineveh shall be destroyed!

Bruuuummm!
Woe! Woooeeee!

What! the drinks?—and the lays?
Yes! everything we once enjoyed!

Bruuuummm!
Woe! Woooeeee!

The bars on Shalmanazar Street
will close as in the summer heat!

The traffic under Sargon's Gate
will dwindle to an alley-cat!

Bruuuummm!
Woe! Woooeeee!

Not a trick, nary one,
all the way to Babylon!

Curtain

Scene Two

Jonah alone before the curtain.

JONAH I admit I'm flattered by the way these folks have taken me into their hearts and lives. A prophet is without honor only in his own country. I suppose I could complain —like somebody else—that when I show them their plain duty, they reply that my style is charming. But who doesn't like to be congratulated on his style? And these people are connoisseurs. Especially that little girl who thinks that King David is—too much. You know, all my life I have felt a little ashamed of my country accent. Especially when I read Isaiah or Ezekiel. But God, blessed be His name, chooses whom He will, even if I was born in Gath-Hepher! Why should I lie? There is no personal satisfaction in the whole of existence like hearing your very words in a popular song sung on the streets! "Yet forty forty forty days—" it *is* catchy. Maybe I ought to be sad— maybe I am sad—that these youngsters give such a superficial response. What did I expect? If people respond on a certain level to everything else, why should they respond differently to this, just because it is a matter of life and death? No—*especially* when it is a matter of life and death. Also, I have to make allowances for these Gentiles. They are such *nice* people. But suppose I reserve judgment until I have seen this remarkable King.

(*Exit*)

The court. The KING *is in his middle twenties, earnest, sweet, humorless, with horn-rimmed spectacles, a Ph.D. in physics. The councilors are again adolescents.*

COURTIER   He is sitting on the edge of his chair again.

DUCHESS   It means he is thinking again.

DUKE   Thinking? It's nothing but indolence. This lazy son of a bitch has replaced war by speculation. Naturally he has nervous fits.

COURTIER   Do you think he would do better to make war, like the late lamented?
(*The* DUKE *doesn't answer*)

DUCHESS   *I* think there is a colossal power in the quiet of our affairs. It's a dynamic equilibrium. "Dynamic equilibrium"—that's good.
      If he should raise his hand,
      if he should flash his eye!
      Who turns his eye away
      and thinks no more of it—
Whoosh! What a man! . . . And what do *you* think of the new bas-relief?

DUKE   The Lion Hunt? Well, look, this one is my paternal grandfather. I like the modeling of the knees, like a clenched fist, eh? But why in hell did the artist make him like he had a toothache?

DUCHESS   Oh, my dear! . . . Hush, he wants to speak.

173

KING Milords and ladies! Don't you think we're in a rut?

DUKE Yes.

KING It's this fuckin' Imperial style! We grind out everything the same. Everywhere I walk in the street, I hear the people muttering, "There's nothing new under the sun." Then what the hell are we supposed to do now?

DUKE (*To his circle*) There! I told you so.

KING (*Passionately*) Put it this way. When I proclaimed the New Imperial Policy, the Nip, and gathered the arts of Egypt, the science of Sumeria, the Babylonian laws, Hebrew music and the psychosexuality of Syria, why, I figured that with such a lot of communications there'd be a lot of feedback. And instead, the fact is, there *is* nothing new under the sun. And what the hell are we supposed to do now?

LADY (*Cries out*) Oh! when I hear that man thinking—he penetrates me. I'm fainting!
      (*She faints*)

DUCHESS Your Majesty, it's insane! We'll call it the Broken Record:
      There's nothing new under the sun!
      What in hell do we do now?
      There's nothing new under the sun,
      so what in hell do we do now?
      (*She claps her hands*)
      There's nothing nothing nothing new—
      What in hell should we do?

KING (*Petulant*) I don't get the joke . . . What's *that*?

ACT FOUR

(*A loud noise off stage: Bruuuuummmm! "Yet Nine and Thirty Days! And Nineveh shall be destroyed!" "Woe! Wooooeee!"*)

COURTIER The people have a new routine, Your Majesty.
(*Enter* JONAH)

LADY (*Recovering from her faint*) Here is that new wit I was telling you about! Nobody talks of anything else.

JONAH Yet thirty-nine days and Nineveh shall be destroyed.
(*The* KING *leaps to his feet and snaps his fingers in triumph*)

KING I've got it! Doom!

JONAH Yet nine and thirty days!

DUKE Look here, foreigner, what do you mean coming into Nineveh like this and exciting the populace without authorization? In twenty-four hours you can become a citizen and get a cabaret license—but do you have to raise such a hullabaloo on the streets? Everywhere I go I hear nothing but Jonah! Jonah!

JONAH I beg your pardon—

DUCHESS Oh, listen to this, he's priceless at debate.

JONAH What I say happens to be true, and I am authorized by the Lord God, Creator of the heavens and the earth.

DUKE So what? It may be true. If true, it's even important. But do you have to start off, on the very first day of your arrival, with such a gloomy prophecy?

JONAH For God's sake, it has to have *some* defect. It's true, it's important, you want it should be jolly to hear as well? My good friend, you remind me of a little story—

DUCHESS What did I tell you? Tell us the story, Jonah— (*They crowd around*)

JONAH It seems there was a *shatchan*—

DUKE A shotgun?

JONAH A *shatchan* is a marriage broker, and he's trying to palm off a Miss Rosalsky. "But she has cross-eyes!" the boy objects. "Cross-eyes! *Each* eye can see a perfect twenty-twenty." "But she limps!" "Limps? Listen, my boy, take my advice. Supposing she never *had* a broken leg, then you're always afraid she might fall off a horse. Here you have a finished product." "She has a hump!" "For God's sake, son, she has to have *some* blemishes." (*Laughter*)

KING Silence! . . . My father—

JONAH Yes, my son.

KING Is it sure what you here proclaim, that in thirty-nine days my city will be destroyed?

JONAH (*Quietly*) It is sure. Yes. (*Smiling*) *Absolutely* sure? No.

KING But from what evidence do you draw this startling conclusion?

JONAH I have it on the authority of the Lord of Hosts.

KING Ah. And what is your criterion for the authority of this Lord?

JONAH A good question. He speaks to me when I am unwilling to listen. He urges on me what I am set against doing. Yet here I am. He has the necessity of actuality.

KING That's a strong authority, and we ought to take Him seriously into account. Is it possible to get him here for a conference? Maybe the best would be a panel discussion; what do you think?

JONAH No, child. He may never be seen, as you are now seeing me. He doesn't take part in panel discussions.

KING Ah. That's a hang-up. Ah, so. (*There is a pause. Sudden decision. The* KING *rises*) My lords! There is probably a good deal in what this scholar alleges. I myself have seen signs and portents in my heart. Therefore let us repent and prepare for this fatal day, which I have now set down on the calendar for the twelfth of next month—

ASTROLOGER The thirteenth, Your Majesty. Thirty-one days hath May.

KING Thank you, the thirteenth. (*Formally*) I hereby proclaim the Perfected Imperial Policy—

ALL The Pip!

KING

> I myself shall rise from my throne and lay my robe from me,
> I shall cover myself with sackcloth and sit in ashes.
> Let neither man nor beast, herd nor flock, taste anything; let them not feed nor drink water.
> But let man and beast be covered with sackcloth and cry mightily unto God.

Yea, let them turn every one from his evil way and
from the work of his hands.

Who can tell if God will turn and repent, and turn
away from his fierce anger, that we perish not.

(*All but* JONAH *kneel*)

KING (*Briskly*)   A committee is formed to finalize these ar-
rangements. I trust that Jonah will give us the benefit of
his long experience and be the chairman. Father, my arm!

Curtain

Scene Four

Outside the walls of Nineveh. Two large calendars are on the wall, numbered from forty to zero. On one, the numbers are crossed out down to ten. The other still has the eleven. Two soldiers march energetically across the scene.

SOLDIERS

Hep! hep! hep! hep!
Forced marches! forced marches!
(*A gloomy ballet of four or five* DANCERS. *They are covered with sackcloth. They paint out the eleven on the calendar. They paint a black stripe on a face*)

SINGER

The suns that daily rise, how soon
have daily more rapidly begun
    like fireballs to pass
    and flicker in a blinding flash!

Thanks be to God, we are aware
that daylight has an end, and are
    composing the hour that remains
    into a kind of dance.
(*The cow, draped in black, is led across. A scuttle of ashes: business of pouring it on the heads of all*)

DANCER   Son of a bitch! These ashes are too hot again!

ANOTHER DANCER   The coals of fire are now mixed with the ashes.

DANCER   Hush! Here comes His Grace.

179

JONAH

ANOTHER DANCER   No hush! It says in the Bible, "Put not your faith in Princes!"
(Enter DUKE, with a little golden scuttle)

DUKE   O my people! These are the ashes of my paternal grandfather, the victor of En-gedi Plain. If he could behold this melancholy scene—his oaken heart would split. But—all flesh is as the grass. I therefore scatter these ashes on my bald head. *(Loud)* Yet ten days and Nineveh shall be destroyed.

SOLDIERS   *(Marching across the scene)*
Hep! hep! hep! hep!
Forced marches! forced marches!
(Enter LADY, busily reading instructions from a brick)

LADY   "In order to rend garments, prepare little cuts with a scissors along the seam." Good. And now I rend them!
(She rends, and all wail. Enter JONAH busily with a hammer, nails and boards. He begins to construct a little booth. Loud hammering. The DANCERS help along)

JONAH   Well! I have come to sit and wait outside the walls of Nineveh that great city to see what will become of Nineveh, that great city.

DUKE   What are you doing, prophet?

JONAH   *(Hammering)*   I am building a little booth to sit in.

DUKE   *(Almost in tears)*   Why are you building a booth *here*, outside the walls of the city? No, don't tell me, don't tell me.

JONAH   I have come to sit outside the walls, to see what will become of Nineveh that great city.

DUKE Why are you lying to me? You tell me that you have come outside to see what will become of Nineveh my city, because you think that *I* will think you have come out here just to get away from the heat. But *I* know that you have come to sit outside the walls to watch what will become of Nineveh, my city!

JONAH Maybe you're right. (*The booth takes form*) See, it's a little housey. I'll go inside a moment and try it out. (*He does*) It's very nice. Do you want to try it?

DUKE (*Slowly*) Look! There is an endless plain, and on it stands nothing but a wooden booth, in the sun and in the wind. What are these great hills? You might imagine they are natural hills of stone. But if you dig there, you will find—Nineveh. Shapeless hills—against the sky. (JONAH *hammers a finishing touch*) Prophet! We are not an unsophisticated people. We do not set a high value, not too high a value, on our Empire City, which is what it is. Yet such as it is, such as it is, such as it is.

JONAH As for me, He bade us to dwell in booths, so that we might leave in a moment, in the night. My booth is finished. On the doorpost, I will nail up an amulet containing the words "Hear, O Israel" in accordance with the injunction, "Thou shalt place them upon the doorposts of thy house and upon thy gates." Here is the doorpost. Here are the words. (*He hammers*) Blest art Thou who has commanded us to nail up the amulet!

SOLDIERS (*Marching across the scene*)
Hep! hep! hep! hep!
Forced marches! forced marches!

Curtain

ACT FIVE

Scene One

Before the curtain. COURTIER *and a* NINEVITE, *wagering.*

COURTIER I'll give you even money.

NINEVITE Even money! Do you think I'm off my conk? You'd think that metropoles like Nineveh were destroyed every other day!

COURTIER What odds do you want?

NINEVITE Ten to one.

COURTIER You're joking. Why, the way things are I wouldn't give you ten to one that the sun will rise to-morrow.

NINEVITE Is that so? I'll give *you* ten to one that the sun will rise.

COURTIER The more fool you. They've seen *spots* on the sun, did you know that? If you stood at court, the way I do, you wouldn't be so god-damned sure about the state that the world's in.

NINEVITE Who the hell is willing to *bet* that Nineveh will be destroyed, you or me? I happen to have faith in this Jew—that's my hunch, see? I'm willing to back it up— money talks, see? But you're not even willing to admit that what he says is unusual.

COURTIER Unusual? I don't know. It's happened before.

NINEVITE   Yeah? When?

COURTIER   (*Counting on his fingers*)   Well, take Babylon—

NINEVITE   Oh, *that*. You know what that was—

COURTIER   What about the Tower?

NINEVITE   There you go again, Babylon, Babylon! *They* always ran in bad luck.

COURTIER   What about the Universal Flood?

NINEVITE   (*Abashed*)   True . . . the Universal Flood . . . There *was* the Universal Flood . . . Has anything been noticed queer about the rivers lately? (*Decisive*) I'll tell you, give me three to one.

COURTIER   Done! Three she sits, one she burns. Now, how much?
> (*Enter* MESSENGER)

MESSENGER   Gentlemen! the Odds Imperial have been posted—

COURTIER   The OI!

NINEVITE   Spill! What's the arithmetic?

MESSENGER   Seven to five against Jonah!

NINEVITE   What did I tell you?

COURTIER   Seven to five! All bets are off. I wouldn't touch it with a ten-foot pole.
> (*Exeunt*)

Scene Two

The KING's *study. The* KING *is leaning against the window, heavily disconsolate.* JONAH *enters merrily singing, notices the* KING *and stops.*

JONAH   Friend! You're sad.
   (*The* KING *shakes him off*)

JONAH   I'm sorry for you.

KING   Are you sorry for me, father?

JONAH   Yes, son.
   (*At this the* KING *bursts into tears.* JONAH *is at a loss*)

JONAH   Say! Let me tell you a little story.

KING   (*Willing to co-operate*)   Sure. I might as well pass the time this way as any other. Only—

JONAH   Only? Laugh! Laugh—God won't be offended.

KING   No, I'm afraid that *you'll* be offended. I never see the point of a joke and never know when I'm supposed to laugh. I guess I have no sense of humor.

JONAH   I'll explain everything! The joke is about Mendele —Mendele Lefkowitz. Oh, he was a disgrace in our town —a loafer—a regular bum.

KING   What—are there Jewish bums?

JONAH   Of course; why not?

KING   Nothing. I didn't think that there were Jewish bums.

JONAH   Believe me, he was a bum. And finally we had enough and the committee came to Mendele and said, "Mendele, we're going to give you a job." "A job!" cried Mendele. "I'm a sick man! How can I hold a job?" "Don't worry, Mendele, don't worry. This is an easy job. Here is a horn, and all you have to do is blow on the horn." "A horn!" cried Mendele. "Me? With my lungs? I've got the consumption and they're asking me to blow on a horn." "Mendele, Mendele! It's not what you think. You're going to be the *Messiah*-blower, so when Messiah comes, you should blow on this horn!"

KING   Messiah? Who's he?

JONAH   Messiah? Messiah—the Messiah is a king.

KING   A king? I'm a king. What's so great about a king, to blow on a horn?

JONAH   Oh, but Your Majesty, Messiah is a *special* king. He is the king of Peace and Justice—he will be king over all mankind.

KING   (*Flat*)   Oh. So what's the joke?

JONAH   (*Passionate*)   "Mendele, Mendele—five thousand years the Messiah hasn't come; you don't have a very hard job." "With *my* luck," said Mendele, "Messiah will come tomorrow."
    (*Long silence*)

KING   (*Puzzled*)   Is that all? I still don't see the joke.

JONAH   Don't you see, boy? Messiah is *everybody*'s luck,

185

yours and mine, forever and ever. And Mendele is worrying about having to work.

(*Pause. Suddenly* JONAH *begins to bawl*)

KING Oh! I get it!
(*And he bursts out laughing*)

Curtain

SCENE THREE

Before the curtain. Enter FIRST SPY, *running, in rags.*

FIRST SPY They're coming! They're coming! Slam the gates.

SECOND SPY Who's coming?

FIRST SPY The Ninevites, you fool! They're counting off the days, and D-day is the day after tomorrow.

SECOND SPY My friend, take hold of yourself. I thought that we were supposed to take them this round.

FIRST SPY All bets are off. Somebody tipped them wise. They're up in arms, eight million people moving like one man. They're throwing coals in the air mixed with fire, and they have put on black camouflage to attack by night.

SECOND SPY What are you talking about? You said it was taking candy from a baby.

FIRST SPY Forced marches day and night! Our fat friend has lost forty pounds.

SECOND SPY You're kidding.

FIRST SPY I'm a changed man myself. I've seen a whole people become serious, and it's a terrible sight.
    (*Exeunt*)

A little scene on one side, lit by a candle. The KING *is kneeling in prayer.*

KING (*Soliloquy*) Let me pray. In the name of the Mother and the Baby, amen. I confess that now that the night has arrived, the last night, I have lost my enthusiasm for this debacle. To yearn for disaster on a determinate day is a childish kind of despair; one does not need the wisdom of the East to think it up. Why? Why? I am still looking for the fascination of a good reason. I *want* to come around to what, in the ordinary course of pleasure and business, I would never have chosen. The fact is that, try as I will, I simply cannot convince myself that Nineveh ought to be destroyed. It's not by a vulgar prejudice that I'm asking for a few more days on earth. To be precise, I don't see as yet that we in *particular* ought to atone so drastically. Oh, we have good cause to repent—everybody does; I understand this a lot better since Jonah came. But this general principle fails to bring me to the proposition that just Nineveh just today must be destroyed. Why is this night different from all other nights? All right, let it be the ultimate night! One ultimate night would be like another anyway, and there must always be a last night. How is it with myself on this night? Beginning with adolescence, I suppose, I was yearning for disaster day by day, the way a man carries poison in his ring. Now that's behind me. Tonight I find it hard to concentrate the peace of mind to be aware of *what* I want. I never used to know where my power ought to strike. Now I have ceased to feel that I have any power at all. Well, there is my prayer. May the words of my mouth and the meditations of my heart be acceptable to Thee, O Lord. (*Pause. The* ANGEL *appears*)

ANGEL Your Majesty—

KING Who is it? (*Courteously*) Please, in this extremity you oughtn't to disturb me. And why aren't you also on your knees, as was commanded? If not now, my friend, when?

ANGEL Let me ask you the same question, if not now, Your Majesty, when? (*The* KING *bows to the ground.* ANGEL, *impatient*) Stand up, boy, stand up. (*The* KING *remains prostrate*) We have listened to the words of your mouth and the meditations of your heart. They are not altogether acceptable. Stand up, I say.
    (*The* KING *rises to his knees*)

KING I know. I wish that I could speak, as I ought, of God and the Angels and the Holy Things. But I have an empirical mind and I can only tell the truth, about my desires and so forth.

ANGEL But you *don't* tell your desire. *What* is it you want? Why don't you stand up and speak out?

KING (*Boldly*) I'd get up, Angel, if I could talk to you as an equal face to face. I'm not. I can't. (*Pause. Still kneeling*) *If*—excuse me, but I must still talk in this hypothetical way—you will understand that it is a time to pick one's words carefully—*if*, I say, if I could see what it is that my people are to repent of (leave me out), do you think we would not accept the consequences? What kind of people do you think we are? But what? Is it our little experiments, always within the possibilities of the natural world, that the Creator of the natural world has found to condemn?

ANGEL   This reasoning is not satisfactory. You yourself said that you have come to a dead stop; you don't know *what* you want; you don't tell me because you can't. "There's nothing new under the sun! What in hell am I supposed to do now!" . . . Have you no answer to this, or must *I* answer, with a large hand?

KING (*Sharply*)   What do *you* want? Do you want me to beg you to let me live? I won't! Let me tell you this (*He rises to his feet and speaks diplomatically*): I am speaking to the ambassador of an absolute power. He has—as you have so well expressed it—a large hand. You understand, this makes dialogue a little difficult—He anticipates me before I have even thought it up. Nevertheless. Let me ask His Holy Name one question: How, in such a doubtful case as this—I mean doubtful to me, of course—is He willing to *commit* Himself? If I were in His shoes—

ANGEL   I beg your pardon—

KING   I think that I would delegate authority. I'd let us work this thing through on our own.
    (*The* ANGEL *roars with laughter. The* KING *falls on his face*)

ANGEL   Innocent boy! You really don't have an inkling of what it means to be damned, do you?

KING (*Looking up*)   No—frankly—I don't.

Curtain

*Outside the walls. Loud laughter. A blinding day. A crowd.
A calendar is torn. All the numbers are crossed out. JONAH's
booth is shut tight.*

NINEVITE (*Pounding on the booth*) Hi, Jonah! Come out!
Come out!

ANOTHER NINEVITE We don't hold our good luck against
you.

NINEVITE What's he afraid of?

ANOTHER NINEVITE (*Mopping his brow*) Is it ever hot!

NINEVITE Was I ever scared!

ANOTHER NINEVITE You telling me? I was shitting green.

COURTIER I was so frightened, my dears, that my wig turned
white.

NINEVITE Forty days!

LADY Whew! The heat, my lord.

DUKE Something formidable. Dammit! You would have
thought it would be a pleasant day to let off steam instead
of just letting off steam. Hee hee.

SEVERAL
We—want—Jonah!
We—want—Jonah!

LADY Maybe he's committed hara-kiri. What a shame!

COURTIER You don't think that *he* believed that story?

DUKE   Why not? Why else? He didn't stand to make a penny by it—unless it was just to attract attention to himself. But how long could it last?

LADY   Really, I'm becoming alarmed. (*She raps*) Jonah, do come out.

NINEVITE   (*Ear to wall*)   Aw, he's alive. I can hear him.

SEVERAL   Hi, Jonah!

LADY   I think you're all horrid. Here Jonah came all the way from Palestine to put on a good show, and now you're shouting at him just when he wants to catch up on his sleep.

NINEVITE   (*Ear to door*)   He ain't sleeping.

ALMOST ALL
     We—want—Jonah!

ONE   Jonah pulled a boner!

ALMOST ALL
     We—want—Jonah!
     Jonah pulled a boner!

LADY   (*Loyally*)   No, no. Jonah, you're a trouper!

SEVERAL   (*At the top of their lungs*)
     JONAH!
     The bars on Shalmanazar Street
     will close as in the summer heat—

DUKE   For God's sake, don't mention the heat! I'm going in.

LADY   So am I, away from these brutes.

COURTIER Your arms, my ladies.
(*The nobles troop off*)

NINEVITE What a sport! He won't even give us the satisfaction. (*Shouts*) Jonah is a lousy loser!

ANOTHER Let's go.

Not a trick, nary one,
all the way to Babylon.
(*Exeunt. Pause.* JONAH *finally pokes his head out*)

JONAH Nu. So it wasn't destroyed. (*He emerges*) If I'd a known, I'd a stood in bed . . . (*He examines the calendars*) Hallelujah! I have been the first prophet to the Gentiles! I'm glad I never gave them something to rue the day. A trouper! All the way from Palestine! "Oh, I think you're horrid." In the name of the Father and the Son, a comedian. It's blinding hot! (*In tears*) What am I doing here tricked out like a horse, like an ambassador? (*Takes off his chain*) The ambassador of the absolute Power. Good-bye, Ambassador! (*Rips his coat*) When somebody is buried, we Jews tear our coats. (*He rips his shirt*) The first prophet to the Gentiles!
(*Pause*)

VOICE OF THE ANGEL Man! Doest thou well to be angry?

JONAH (*Wheeling about*) You! you—!
(*And he says in a choked and gasping voice*)
Wasn't it what I *said*
when I was yet at home?
Therefore I *fled*
Because I *knew*
Thou art a *gracious* God,

merciful, slow to anger,
of great loving kindness,
and Thou *repentest*
of the evil.

Now therefore *take*,
I *beg* You,
my life from me.
For it is better for me to die
than to live.
(*He falls in a faint. Enter the* ANGEL)

ANGEL

All bad breaks are symbols, save
the fact in which these creatures live
    that only slowly in time
    reveals its calamitous name.

In the name of the Holy Ghost, spring up,
Thou tree of Delusory Hope
    whose roots are bathing in the ic-
    y streams that flow through Paradise.
(*And he draws from the earth a plant of luxuriance
whose leafy boughs he tenderly disposes above the
place where* JONAH *is fainted. Depending from this
tree is a kind of watermelon. Exit. Enter a* WORM *and
says*)

WORM

I am a little worm
and I follow him about
wherever he does go
I follow him in and out.

194

Wherever he comes out
I shortly enter there:
this Angel, it is Hope,
this worm, it is Despair.
(*The* WORM *hides behind the tree.* JONAH, *reviving, lies flat and looks up surprised*)

JONAH   How green this ocean is! I didn't think the sailors would throw me into such pleasant waves. I'll float a moment here. (*Agitated*) Swim! Swim! (*He tries to swim*) No! One moment more—lie here—and catch my breath. (*He sits bolt upright*) It's a tree . . . Very nice. (*Leans on his elbow*) Cool. Delicate. It's refreshing. Birds, too? I'm a connoisseur of bird calls; I can call them (*Whistles*)—they don't always come. (*Coos*) Hello, little little pigeon! . . . I remember it all. It is the wall of Nineveh that great city. Blinding hot! *This* is strange. (*He puts his hand out into the light*) Ouch! Hot! It's still hot. Well, I am used, a prophet of the Lord of Hosts, to come on these unexpected gentle blessings. (*Weeps*) Don't cry. What's to cry about? It's with consolation I'm crying. (*In highest delight*) A watermelon! With a spigot and glasses! How convenient! (*Draws and drinks, enraptured*) Blessed art Thou, O Lord, Creator of the fruit of the soil. (*Drinks again*) World! World! I pledge you the water of Paradise!

   (A NINEVITE *comes by cautiously*)

NINEVITE   Jonah?

JONAH   Come in! Come in!

NINEVITE   Why—that's a fine tree you have.

JONAH   Isn't it?

NINEVITE For heaven's sake, cool! (*Eagerly*) What's that you're drinking?

JONAH Taste it! No—don't say a word. Just taste it!

NINEVITE Well (*Drinks*)—In the name of Essarhaddon, more! (*They drink another round. The* NINEVITE *tenders his glass*) Jonah, I don't like to sponge on you again, but—

JONAH Drink! Drink! You remind me of the *schnorrer*—

NINEVITE Whazza snorer?

JONAH The beggar. He comes to the merchant's house just when the other *schnorrer* is leaving. "Don't go in today," says his friend, "the old gent's in a bad mood; he won't give you more than a dollar." "Nonsense! Why should I save *him* a dollar—is he making *me* any presents?"
(*Pause*)

NINEVITE (*Bashful*) Jonah—

JONAH Yes, boy.

NINEVITE This is a keen thing you have here . . . When I tell the others, who will believe me? Could I bring a friend, a witness?

JONAH Bring! bring! Bring them all.
(*Exit* NINEVITE. *Immediately a large crowd gathers. General racket and drinking*)

JONAH Come in! Welcome! It's air-conditioned.

COURTIER Air-conditioned? It knocks you flat. I feel a consumption coming on.

NINEVITE   I pledge you a glass of the water of Paradise!
(*He keels over*)

SEVERAL   A toast! a toast!

LADY   I knew that our Jonah would top off his performance
with an encore.

JONAH (*Proposing a toast*)   To the Whale!

COURTIER   Whale! Whale!

JONAH   To *The Glory of Tammuz*.

DUKE   I give you *The Glory of Tammuz*.

JONAH   Ladies and gentlemen, to my wife!

LADY   Oh, Jonah! Isn't marriage something?

NINEVITE   His Imperial Majesty is coming.

ALL   Him! Him!
(*With a mighty roar an east wind rushes across the
scene. There is a crack of thunder. Blacks and lights.
The branches are torn. The multitude vanishes. The*
WORM *stabs the melon*)

WORM   Die, Melon!
(*It explodes.* JONAH *is knocked flat. Blackout. Blinding heat as he comes to. Around him are the rem-
nants of rejoicing. He sits up, staring forward. The*
ANGEL *appears and stands behind him*)

ANGEL (*quietly*)   Jonah.
(JONAH *shrugs*)

ANGEL   Doest thou well to be angry for the gourd?

JONAH (*Leaping up aggressively*) Yes, I do well to be angry, even unto death.

ANGEL (*With compassion*) Look, Jonah. You take pity on this watermelon, for which you did not labor. You did not make it grow. It sprang up in a moment, and it perished in a moment . . . Should not I spare Nineveh that great city, wherein are eight million persons who, if I may say so, cannot discern between their right hand and their left, and also much cattle? (*After a moment* JONAH *relaxes into a smile*) Nebich?

Curtain

Comment on *Jonah*

This play follows act by act the incidents related in the Book of Jonah. Among the books of the Bible, Jonah is unique as the only comedy, though I suppose a kind of somber irony (if not sarcasm) is pervasive throughout the Bible, since everything occurs on two levels.

The essential situation, the Prophet whose prophecy proves false and who then says to God, "I told you so!" is perfectly comic, and the concluding fable about the folk who "don't know their right hand from their left" is certainly meant to be funny. And it seems to me that the style also has a genre realism not altogether serious, e.g., "he found a ship going to Tarshish and he paid the fare."

The perplexity in the book is the motive of Jonah's flight. The reason given in IV:2 must of course be accepted: "Was not this my saying?"—that Nineveh would be spared —"*therefore* I fled." But what does it mean? Simple pique at having been made a fool of? Or perhaps, Jonah disapproves of God's repenting? I prefer to put it all together as a conflict of compassion and rage: the wise man flees from his wisdom—in the world—as it is. Look for this within the soul and you find the little old man who tells Jewish jokes and is always angry and who wants to die, "for it is better for me to die than to live."

The range of speech given to the old man, from marriage-broker jokes to meditations on first theology, is not far-fetched; I once knew such a person myself. I think that

Jonah should have a slight Jewish accent throughout, but his syntax rises and falls with the subject. As to the jokes, connoisseurs will recognize which ones I have lifted from Lou Holtz, which from Sigmund Freud, and so forth. But I assume that they were all told on the way to Tarshish and are in the public domain.

The mores of Nineveh I have simply borrowed from the principle of Mandeville's *Fable of the Bees*: Private Vices are Public Benefits. If adopted with a good conscience, this principle would give us a guileless and rather childlike society; it might be, all things considered, the best option for our own Empire City.

Performance has shown that it is best to double and triple the cast of characters wherever possible. For indeed Jonah meets the *same* people in every situation, on the ship, in the whale, and in Nineveh.

This is the first play I have written for a long time and I have learned what it is I love in the theatre. It is the glorification of simple overt acts, like hitting one another with the furniture or sitting down together to a cup of coffee or carrying on a conversation. In place of the enormous interior scene of novels or the exterior scope of cinema, it is good to rely on the finite physical reality of a few people on a little stage.

New York City
January 1942

PAUL GOODMAN, a native New Yorker, was born in 1911. After graduating from City College in New York, he received his Ph.D. in humanities from the University of Chicago. Mr. Goodman has taught at the University of Chicago, New York University, Black Mountain College, Sarah Lawrence, the University of Wisconsin, and has lectured widely at various universities throughout the country. He is associated with the New York and Cleveland institutes for Gestalt Therapy and the University Seminar on the City at Columbia. He is also a Fellow of the Institute for Policy Studies in Washington, D.C.

Mr. Goodman has written for *Commentary, Politics, Kenyon Review, Resistance, Liberation, Partisan Review,* etc. His fiction includes *The Facts of Life, The Break-Up of Our Camp, Parents' Day, The Empire City,* and *Making Do,* and he has also published a volume of verse, *The Lordly Hudson. Kafka's Prayer* and *The Structure of Literature* are books of criticism. In the area of social studies, in addition to being the co-author of *Communitas* and *Gestalt Therapy,* he has written *Art and Social Nature, Growing Up Absurd, Utopian Essays and Practical Proposals, Drawing the Line* (a pamphlet), *Community of Scholars, Compulsory Mis-Education,* and *People or Personnel.*

Mr. Goodman is married and has three children.